Inspecting and the Inspectorate

by John Blackie

*Part-time Lecturer in Education and English,
Homerton College, Cambridge;
formerly H.M. Inspector of Schools*

LONDON

ROUTLEDGE & KEGAN PAUL

First published 1970
by Routledge & Kegan Paul Ltd
Broadway House, 68-74 Carter Lane
London, E.C.4
Printed in Great Britain
by Northumberland Press Limited
Gateshead

ISBN 7100 6780 1 (c)

THE STUDENTS LIBRARY OF EDUCATION has been designed to meet the needs of students of Education at Colleges of Education and at University Institutes and Departments. It will also be valuable for practising teachers and educationalists. The series takes full account of the latest developments in teacher-training and of new methods and approaches in education. Separate volumes will provide authoritative and up-to-date accounts of the topics within the major fields of sociology, philosophy and history of education, educational psychology, and method. Care has been taken that specialist topics are treated lucidly and usefully for the non-specialist reader. Altogether, the Students Library of Education will provide a comprehensive introduction and guide to anyone concerned with the study of education, and with educational theory and practice.

This book, by a former member of Her Majesty's Inspectorate, is in the main an account of the present functions, duties and powers of the Inspectorate, their relations with the D.E.S., with the L.E.A.s and with teachers. This is prefaced by a brief historical account in Chapter 2 of the development of the Inspectorate from the first appointments in 1839. Some knowledge of this history is all the more necessary because of the traumatic effect on the relations between H.M.I.s and teachers of the Revised Code of 1862. This for nearly forty years turned the H.M.I. into a kind of Lord High Executioner, and reduced his former varied functions to a single judgemental one, and a very lowly and circumscribed form of judgement too. The process was degrading for both H.M.I.s and teachers (as the cynical Mr Lowe intended it should be) and it gave rise to a body of myths about

Inspectors, traces of which still remain, as Mr Blackie shows in Chapter 3.

The wider functions of the Inspectorate have long been restored and extended and how these operate in the schools of today, as seen from inside the Inspectorate, is the subject of this book. How the teacher sees it is another matter, of special concern to the young teacher, in most cases not too sure of his own judgement and in need of counsel. Certainly this book should help him to distinguish between reality and fantasy in his relationship with the Inspectorate and enable him to benefit from the visit of the H.M.I. to his classroom.

J. W. TIBBLE

Contents

CONTENTS

Preface

This book is based on the experience of thirty-three years as a member of Her Majesty's Inspectorate of Schools, years for me of uninterrupted interest and happiness. The debts of gratitude I have incurred are too numerous and various to mention here. I would like to utter my general thanks to the many colleagues with whom I have worked, and who have been my friends, from my joining the inspectorate as a very young and ignorant recruit in 1933 to my leaving it as its senior member in 1966. For the historical sections I have drawn heavily upon the work of Miss Nancy Ball, Dr E. L. Edmonds and Mr H. E. Boothroyd, to whom reference is made in the text. I am grateful also to the Department of Education and Science for allowing me to make use of my official experience and to Her Majesty's Stationery Office for permission to print in full the Select Committee's Report on the Inspectorate and the Department's observations thereon.

1

Why have inspectors?

The functions of inspectors of schools have been in the past, and still are, very varied. It is broadly speaking true that inspectorates have always been established, and in many cases are still maintained, in order to provide some assurance for the taxpayer that his money is being properly spent. Just how this phrase 'properly spent' is interpreted varies widely. In an authoritarian country it will be defined as 'spent on the teaching of the curriculum precisely as laid down by the government', and even in many democracies, this definition would not be altogether inaccurate. In the United Kingdom much is left to the judgement and discretion of the inspector. In the former case the inspector is there to see that things are done in a particular way; in the latter to decide whether what is being done is being done well. Yet there is probably no inspectorate that is confined to this basic function, and even the basic function itself, as we have just seen, varies much in the way it is interpreted.

It is sometimes asked whether the very existence of a school inspectorate, quite apart from its function, is not an affront to the teaching profession. This is a fair question which needs a fair answer. When H.M. Inspectorate was established in 1839 the claim of teachers to be regarded as professionals was without any basis. Training scarcely existed. Graduates were not found in the elementary schools, to which the inspectors were then confined, and many teachers were grossly ignorant and even illiterate. Inspection was then certainly no affront, nor was this, so far as I know, ever asserted. But in 1968, when the great majority of teachers are trained and a substantial minority possess University degrees, the question has real point.

The answer is sometimes based upon a claim for the dignity of the profession. But assertions about dignity are essentially emotional, and though they may indicate the existence of strong feelings, are not of much value as arguments. Such assertions sometimes provoke the statement that no other profession is inspected and that inspection is inconsistent with being a profession at all. As a matter of literal fact this is not true. The fighting forces are all inspected and most other professions, though they do not use the term 'inspector' are so structured that something like inspection is involved in their make-up. Even if this were not so, it could still be argued that the teaching of children is properly treated as a very special case, since they have little or no choice of who is to teach them, while even their parents' rights in this matter are in most cases apparent rather than real.

All this kind of argument is in fact irrelevant. The only sensible approach to the matter is to ask whether the functions of inspectors, as they are now, are useful to teachers, whether they are carried out in such a way as to be acceptable to them. Also, of course, whether their aims and methods can be improved. These questions provide a basis for discussion and I shall return to them in chapters four and five.

Even if answers favourable to the inspectorate were forthcoming from the teaching force, it might still be questioned whether the inspectorate in its present form is adapted to the needs and conditions of today. H.M. Inspectorate was, at its foundation and for many years of its existence, essentially a body of gentlemen appointed to look after the education of the poor by the lower middle class. Has it adapted itself to the social patterns of the later twentieth century? Are its membership and its organization what schools and teachers now need? How does it fit in with institutions which have come into being long after itself, the Institutes of Education, the Schools Council? On another tack, is there any place for both national and local Inspectorates? If inspection is necessary, could it not be done entirely by Local Education Authorities? Or by teachers themselves? These are not imaginary questions. They have all been asked at one time or another and some are still being asked, and will be increasingly asked. I shall try to suggest possible answers in the ensuing chapters. If the teaching profession in the past has, on the whole and for most of the time, taken inspection for granted, it is probably less likely to do so in the future, and I hope that the book will provide the young student with the material necessary for making his own assessment of the inspectorate.

2

H.M. and other inspectorates

1839–62

The history of inspection and of the national, local and religious inspectorates is not uninteresting but it is too long to be told in detail here. Miss Nancy Ball's monograph on the first ten years of H.M. Inspectorate and Dr E. L. Edmonds's more general history, to which reference is made in the bibliography, are models of research and readability and my own debt to them is great. In this chapter I shall outline only briefly the development of inspection, with particular emphasis on features which have helped to shape the profile that it displays today.

In the eighteenth century the S.P.C.K. appointed Charity School and Sunday School inspectors and, when the British and Foreign School Society began to establish schools in 1808 and the National Society for Promoting the Education of the Poor in the Principles of the Established Church in 1811, both bodies appointed some inspectors. In 1833 the first grant of public money to education was voted by parliament and for six years it was distributed unconditionally to the two voluntary Societies. By 1839 it was beginning to be felt that the public had a right to know how their money was being spent and to some assurance that it was being, as was said in chapter one,

4

'properly spent'. In April of that year the Committee of the Privy Council on Education was set up, and on 3 June the following minute was issued: 'The Committee recommend that no further grant be made now or hereafter for the establishment or support of normal schools or of any other schools unless the right of inspection be retained . . .', followed, on 24 September, by another minute, which stated that:

> Inspectors, authorized by Her Majesty in Council, will be appointed from time to time to visit schools to be henceforth aided by public money; the Inspectors will not interfere with the religious instruction, or discipline, or management of the school, it being their object to collect facts and information and to report the results of their inspections to the Committee of Council.

In December the Home Secretary, Lord John Russell, appointed the first two H.M. Inspectors, the Rev. John Allen, educated at Westminster and Trinity College, Cambridge, and Mr Hugh Tremenheere, educated at Winchester and New College, of which latter foundation he was, and remained until 1856, a Fellow.

This development did not please everybody. Lord Melbourne disliked it intensely. The Societies saw it as an invasion of their territory, and some of the Bishops felt the same, Durham and Norwich being notable exceptions. Dr Blomfield, the Bishop of London, however, who was 'generally regarded as the most influential churchman of the time, of far greater importance than the Archbishop of Canterbury' (Ball, 1963, 37), and who had begun by being a strong opponent of Government intervention, changed his mind after an interview with Allen and gave it his support. There was a good deal of manoeuvring

5

and compromising and finally, on 15 July 1840, the following concordat was arrived at:

1. That the Archbishops be consulted, each in his province, before the appointment of any Inspector of Anglican schools was recommended; that the Archbishops be at liberty to suggest a name and that none be appointed without their concurrence.
2. That an inspector's appointment could be ended at any time by the Archbishop withdrawing his concurrence.
3. That, in whatever general instructions were issued to inspectors, the Archbishop's instructions as to religious teaching should be incorporated and the whole shown to the Archbishop for comment before being sanctioned.
4. That grants should be proportionate to the number of children educated and the amount of money raised by the voluntary body.
5. That the whole arrangement be submitted as a Minute to Parliament (Ball, 1963, 40).

One of the early consequences of this concordat was that inspection became denominational. In 1847 a similar agreement was made with the Wesleyans and later on with the Roman Catholics, an arrangement which persisted until 1870. Until this later year the great majority of the Anglican inspectors were clergymen, but from 1870 to 1968 no clergymen or ministers of any denomination were appointed, and schools of every denomination were and still are inspected by the same inspectors. The ban on clergymen was lifted in 1968.

In January 1840, when Allen and Tremenheere set out on their first tours of inspection, not much was known of the condition of the elementary schools, and the first useful task which they and the other early inspectors performed was simply to collect information. What they found was for the most part depressing. The monitorial system for which so much had been claimed, and which was favoured in the British (non-conformist) schools, emerged as hopelessly inefficient. The teachers, miserably paid, untrained and uneducated, were just as bad, and attendance, especially in the summer and at harvest time, was too often brief and irregular. The following account of a school by the Rev. the Hon. B. Noel, who was employed as a sort of occasional inspector and was not an H.M. Inspector, is not as untypical as might be hoped:

I found 31 children from 2 to 7 years of age. The room was a cellar about 10 feet square and about 9 feet high. The only window was less than 18 inches square and not made to open. Although it was a warm day towards the end of August, there was a fire burning, and the door, through which alone any air could be admitted, was shut. Of course, therefore, the room was close and hot, but there was no remedy. The damp subterranean walls required, as the old woman assured us, a fire throughout the year. If she opened the door the children would rush out to life and liberty, while the cold blast rushing in would torment her aged bones with rheumatism. Still further to restrain their vagrant propensities and to save them from the danger of tumbling into the fire, she had crammed the children as closely as possible into a dark corner at the foot of her bed. Here they sat, in pestiferous obscurity, totally destitute of books, and without light enough to enable them to read, had books been placed in their hands. Six children out of the thirty,

7

had brought some twopenny books, but these also, having been made to circulate through sixty little hands, were now so well soiled and tattered as to be rather memorials of past achievements than the means of leading the children to fresh exertion. The only remaining instruments of instruction possessed by the dame, who lamented her hard lot . . . were a glass-full of sugar plums . . . on the table . . . and a cane by its side.

There were of course bright exceptions, notably at King's Somborne in Hampshire, where an enlightened parson and his wife encouraged the teachers, and with them produced a school which must have compared favourably with many schools today (Ball, 1963, 99-100). When conditions such as those described by Noel existed at all, let alone in quantity, the first need in the inspectors was fearless and outspoken reporting without minding too much whose toes were trodden on. It was fortunate that the early inspectors exhibited just these qualities. The terms of their appointment gave them some degree of independence from both Government and churches, and many of their reports gave offence in both quarters.

The instructions which were issued to inspectors in 1840, drawn up by Dr Kay (later Sir James Kay-Shuttleworth), contained the following words:

One main object of your visit is to afford them [the parochial clergy and ministers] your assistance in all efforts for improvement in which they may desire your aid: but you are in no respect to interfere with the instruction, management or discipline of the schools, or to press upon them any suggestion that they may be dis-inclined to receive. . . . When a system of inspection aided by public grant is for the first time brought

8

into operation, it is of the utmost consequence that you should bear in mind that this inspection is not intended as a means of exercising control, but of affording assistance; that it is not to be regarded as operating for the restraint of local efforts, but for their encouragement; and that its chief objects will not be attained without the co-operation of the school committees;—the Inspector having no power to interfere, and not being instructed to offer any advice or information excepting where it is invited (Minutes, 1839-40).

These are remarkable words, and correspond to an ideal of individual initiative and local effort which still persists in English education, yet had they been too literally interpreted or given to minor officials, who, with an eye to the job, played for safety, they might have done much harm. Fortunately H.M. Inspectors from the beginning interpreted their duties liberally. Tremenheere was in trouble almost at once. In 1842 he wrote a scathing report on the British Schools in London, which annoyed the committee of the Society so much that they complained to Lord Wharncliffe, the President of the Council, who upheld the inspector who, though he might 'in some particulars, not have been sufficiently careful' had yet acted 'in an anxious desire to do his duty'. Allen was equally outspoken, if more tactful and charitable. There was no holding back of unpalatable information (Ball, 1963, 54).

But the inspectors were not simply report writers. They quickly established the practice of giving constructive advice and encouragement to teachers, and were pioneers of reform and advance. They spread abroad information about successful experiments. They advocated separate

9

classrooms, cloakrooms and good ventilation at a time when these things were regarded as needless extravagances. They encouraged the establishment of infants' schools and mixed schools. They opposed corporal punishment, save as a last resort. They recommended the provision of good books and poetry, the abandonment of rote learning, the use of maps and even geography lessons 'by the side of the nearest river or pond' (Minutes, 1846).

This spirit of independence in inspectors was clearly of great importance to the teachers, who were then more or less unorganized and more or less at the mercy of the School committees. It derived partly from the terms of the Concordat of 1840 but mainly from the inspectors themselves. In 1845 it was reinforced by the refusal of the Lord President (the Duke of Buccleuch) to suppress a report of Allen's which had given offence to the Archbishop of Canterbury and, to look ahead for a moment, in 1863 by a more drastic event. On 12 April of that year 'Lord Robert Cecil moved a resolution in the House of Commons protesting against the alteration of Inspectors' reports by the Department. Lowe, the Vice-President, denied, in good faith, that Inspectors had been instructed to alter their reports; but while he was speaking, an altered report was being circulated round the back benches, with the result that the government was defeated and Lowe resigned' (Boothroyd, 1923, 22). This set the seal upon the educational autonomy of the inspectorate, which has been maintained and jealously guarded ever since.

About the relations between inspectors and teachers in these early years it is not easy to be sure. Information is scanty and comes mainly from the inspectors. The following passage from Miss Ball's book is of great interest:

In judging the inspectors' attitude to teachers, we must remember the contempt with which their trade (it would be anachronistic to call it a profession) was regarded even by persons interested in popular education. There is a revealing comment in a letter from Allen to Kay-Shuttleworth, who had asked advice as to whether he could safely invite his schoolmaster to dine at Gawthorpe: 'About your dinner-party, I am not sure what your clergy would think. . . . We very much need to have different classes brought together; but, although I have met with several instances of the schoolmistress being received at the clergyman's table, I scarcely recollect an instance out of London (except the Dean of Bangor) of a clergyman's shaking hands with or even talking familiarly with, the parochial school master' (Ball, 1963, 220).

Given the structure and assumptions of English society 120 years ago, it would have been ludicrous to expect a body of gentlemen, most of whom had been educated at public schools and at Oxford or Cambridge, to treat elementary school teachers as their social equals, and the independence just referred to included the right, or the assumption of it, to speak very critically of particular teachers in published reports. This undoubtedly aroused justifiable resentment, yet the inspectors were the teachers' champions, 'perhaps the only people in the country', says Miss Ball, 'who knew them individually and as a class and, seeing their weaknesses, recognized the insoluble difficulties they often had to face' (Ball, 1963, 222). There is much evidence that the inspectors regarded the teachers with sympathy and encouraged them actively to form their own associations, and some that their visits and their personal kindness were appreciated.

In 1847 there occurred a development which greatly increased the power of the inspectorate over both schools and teachers. This was the introduction of the pupil-teacher system, under which 'such scholars as might be distinguished by proficiency and good conduct were apprenticed to skilful masters, to be instructed and trained, so as to be prepared to complete their education as school-masters in a normal school' (this latter term, which has practically dropped out of use in England, meant what is now called a college of education). Not only did 'the scholars' have to be examined by H.M. Inspectors before they could become pupil-teachers, but in addition no school was allowed to employ one of them unless H.M. Inspector reported favourably upon it. Furthermore, as no 'normal school' could receive grant unless it applied for inspection (this had been laid down in 1839), the power of H.M. Inspectors was felt here too, and that it was no shadow of power was soon discovered by the Training College at Winchester, when it was turned down by H.M.I. the Rev. H. Moseley, F.R.S., and remained outside the state system for some years (Ball, 1963, 162).

It was obvious that until a sound system of teacher-training could be established the education of children in England could make little progress. H.M. Inspectors had been the means of drawing public attention to the need for such a system. They had emphasized in all their reports the poor quality of the teachers, and, at the same time, had tried to encourage them to improve. It was inevitable that they should play a dominant part in the setting-up of the training system, and its improvement thereafter. They continued to be closely concerned with the examination and assessment of intending teachers far into the twentieth century and are still brought into consultation on matters of probation.

There can be no question of the contribution made by the first inspectors to educational advance. It was recognized at the time and in retrospect it looks even more remarkable. In 1849, ten years after the foundation of the corps, there were only fifteen H.M.I.s in England, together with five who were concerned only with Poor Law Schools. Tremenheere had resigned in 1843, to become H.M. Inspector of Mines, and Allen in 1847, to become Archdeacon of Salop. Of this small body of gentlemen Miss Ball writes, at the conclusion of her book:

Once they had won acceptance as guides and advisers, the Inspectors were in a position to bring about great changes, not only in curriculum and techniques but in the whole approach to the education of the people. The work of the schools was in 1849, by our standards and, indeed, by theirs, still woefully imperfect. Nevertheless H.M. Inspectors, largely by exerting the kind of indirect and unofficial influence of which Lingen spoke, had been instrumental in causing something approaching a revolution in educational aims and methods (Ball, 1963, 241-2).

1862–98

In 1858, one of those national stock-takings of education which have since become a time-honoured custom, was made by a Commission under the chairmanship of the Duke of Newcastle. In 1860 the Commission reported, and their report included the following sentence:

There is only one way of securing this result (the

13

efficient teaching of every child) which is to institute a searching examination by competent authority of every child in every school to which grants are to be paid, with the view of ascertaining whether these indispensable elements of knowledge are thoroughly acquired, and to make the prospects and position of the teacher dependent to a considerable extent on the results of this examination (Newcastle, 1860, 6-156).

These dread words were to affect the whole course of English elementary education and to change radically the function of H.M. Inspectors during the next thirty-six years.

Lowe, the Vice-President of the Council, was far from being in sympathy with the outlook and procedures of the inspectorate and in this he was at one with his predecessor Adderley. They both thought that inspectors had been exceeding their proper functions, that they had been acting independently of the Department's policies, that their reports were 'philosophical disquisitions upon educational theories' and that it was time that their duties were more exactly defined, in short that they were cut down to size. The Newcastle Report gave him exactly what he wanted, and in 1861 he introduced a Code which made the amount of grant payable, and thus of course the amount of the teachers' salaries, dependent upon the results of an examination by H.M. Inspectors of individual children in the three R's. This raised such a storm of protest that, in 1862, a revised Code was issued in which the grants were dependent partly upon the results of examination and partly on attendance. All children over eight were to be examined; one-third of the grant was to depend on attendance and two-thirds upon results. Despite modifications, this Code remained, in its essential features, in force until 1898.

The effect of 'payment by results' upon educational standards was almost entirely deleterious and has been often described elsewhere. The effect upon the inspectorate and upon the relations of inspectors with teachers was equally deplorable. Not all H.M.I.s realized at first that this was bound to be so, and in 1864 the Department claimed that nearly all of them supported the new system. If this was ever true it was certainly not true for long, and H.M.I. Mr Matthew Arnold, from the outset, saw its dangers and was strongly opposed to it. In his Report for 1863 he wrote:

> The inspector hears every child in the groups before him read and, so far, his examination is more complete than the old inspection. But he does not question them and he does not as an examiner . . . go beyond the three matters—reading, writing and arithmetic—and the amount of these three matters which the standards (laid down) themselves prescribed . . . the entries for grammar, geography and history have now altogether disappeared from the forms of the report furnished to the inspector. The nearer, therefore, he gets to the top of the school, the more does his examination in itself become an inadequate means of testing the real attainments and intellectual life of the scholars before him (Arnold, 1908).

By 1869, H.M.I. the Rev. F. Watkins, who had, at the outset, been a supporter of the Revised Code, wrote in his report: 'from the nature of (this) examination, which is entirely formal and mechanical, only mechanical results can be expected' (Edmonds, 1962, 81). The pictorial spirit of independence and habit of fearless reporting remained, fortunately, unimpaired.

Sir James Kay-Shuttleworth, who had by now retired from the Department, wrote in 1862 a strong criticism of the proposed system. Speaking of a putative reduction of grant he says:

> The inspector would have been the ostensible instrument of this reduction. He has hitherto exercised greater influence on the improvement of the schools by his experience and conciliation of co-operative effort, than by his power to recommend the withdrawal of the grants to the teachers and pupil-teachers for neglect and consequent unsatisfactory results, either in organization, instruction or discipline. His time, under the Revised Code, would be consumed in a mechanical drudgery which would necessarily withdraw his attention from the religious and general instruction, and from the moral features of the school. The organization of the school could not be inspected, for it would necessarily be broken up into groups of age for purposes of the examination. Scholars with attainments above the Code standard would be degraded to their groups of age to be placed along with untaught savages, dullards, sluggards and truants unable to reach the standard. The manager and teachers would watch anxiously the trial of each child, which was to determine whether twenty-five shillings or nothing was to be awarded to the school (Kay-Shuttleworth, 1862, 599).

This remarkable prophecy, by the man who had written the first *Instructions to Inspectors* in 1840, was pretty well fulfilled. However hard an inspector tried to look at a school as a whole, he was bound to give his main attention to a mechanical examination. However hard he tried to maintain a civilized relationship with the teachers, he could

not fail to be regarded as an enemy. As Dr Edmonds writes:
'Instead of being a constructive adviser the inspector had
become the harsh dispenser of an all too meagre government grant whose size he determined' (Edmonds, 1962,
81).

The institution of examinations meant a heavy increase
in inspectors' work, and in 1863 a new grade of Assistant
Inspector, with the job of marking exercises, was instituted.
This was important, in that it introduced 'class distinction'
into the inspectorate, which did not disappear until 1944.
The Assistants were headmasters of elementary schools,
chosen, for some years, by individual H.M.I.s. They were
not allowed to examine except in the presence of, or by a
written order from, H.M.I.s and their inferior status was
marked by their appearing in the official list as 'Mr' while
H.M.I.s were 'Esq' (Boothroyd, 1923, 25-2b). Often, it appears, they did most of the work. The legend of H.M.I.
riding up to the school in hunting pink and leaving, after
a few minutes' chat with the head teacher and managers,
to join the hounds, while his Assistant carried out the
examination, described by A. P. Graves (Graves, 1930) indi-
cates the boredom of the whole dreary procedure and the
gulf between H.M.I., Assistant, and Head Teacher. H.M.I.
Mr E. M. Sneyd-Kinnersley, who served throughout the
payment-by-results period, wrote:

as a rule, if we began about 10, we finished about 11.45.
If the master was a good fellow and trustworthy, we
looked over the few papers in dictation and arithmetic,
marked the Examination Schedule, and showed him the
result before we left. Then he calculated his percentage
of passes, his grant and his resulting income; and went to
dinner with what appetite he might. But if the man was
cross-grained and likely to complain that the exercises

17

were too hard, the standard of marking too high, and so on, he would be left in merciful ignorance of the details. Half an hour in the evening sufficed for making up the Annual Report and the incident was closed (Sneyd-Kinnersley, 1908).

The off-hand tone is very different from that of the first inspectors, nearly all of whom were clergymen who saw their work as part of their Christian duty, which many of them according to their lights carried out with true Christian charity.

In 1869, the last clerical H.M.I. was appointed, and in 1870 the Forster Act opened a new era in English education. It necessitated a further increase in H.M. Inspectorate and led to the appointment of local inspectors by some of the larger School Boards and of Diocesan inspectors by the Churches, since, from 1870 to 1944, H.M.I. did not inspect religious teaching. As time went on the Department realized that an H.M.I. must be more than an examiner. In 1878, in the *Instructions to Inspectors* we read:

Their Lordships . . . attach great importance to a second visit (without notice) being made, as far as possible to every school in the year, with a view to the general encouragement of the teachers and the children and to enable you to exercise a larger influence upon the general conduct of the schools than is possible when only one visit for the purpose of examination takes place; and they would strongly impress upon you their desire that you should endeavour to make all your visits, as far as lies in your power, an encouragement and assistance to managers and teachers in their difficult work.

These were fine words, but they could be very little more

than that until the abolition of payment-by-results twenty years later.

We have hitherto been concerned solely with the inspection of elementary schools and colleges of education, but in the last half of the century, the duties of H.M.I.s were extended beyond these two fields. As early as 1851 the inspection of evening schools had begun. In 1853 the Department of Science and Art was established with its own inspectorate, mainly consisting of retired Royal Engineer officers (the only men in the country who had received a sound scientific education). In 1856, this department, which had been attached to the Board of Trade, was transferred to the Education Department and became known as the South Kensington Inspectorate. Slowly and tentatively there was a move towards the inspection of secondary, technical and art education, but it was not until 1898 that a branch of H.M. Inspectorate was formed, responsible for the inspection of secondary schools, technical schools, schools of art, science and art classes in elementary schools, evening classes, pupil-teacher centres and manual instruction in elementary schools, a hybrid organization which survived only for six years. In 1883, the first woman, Miss Emily Jones, had been appointed, not to the inspectorate, but to the post of Directress of Needlework, followed in 1890 by an Inspectress of Cooking and Laundrywork, Miss Harrison. These two appointments were on a temporary experimental basis, but in 1894, the authorities threw caution to the winds and placed the Hon. Mrs Colborne, who had succeeded Miss Jones, on the permanent establishment. It was not, however, until 1896 that women were allowed into Girls and Infants schools for purposes unconnected with housecraft (Boothroyd, 1923, 76). In that year and in 1897, four were appointed for this purpose with the rank of Sub-Inspector. By 1903, there were six such women and in that year Sir Robert Morant appointed the Hon. Maude Lawrence as Chief Woman Inspector with the rank of H.M.I.

The first School Boards to appoint their own inspectors were Sheffield and London. This was in 1872 (Edmonds, 1960, 97-100). Other large cities followed suit, but in 1965 only fifty out of the 164 Local Education Authorities employed their own inspectors (Plowden, 1967, 947). The School Board inspectors were mostly of less elevated social rank than H.M.I.s and were certainly less highly regarded. They had numerous administrative duties and were in many areas maids-of-all-work. They were, however, in closer touch with the teachers during the period under review than many H.M.I.s and some were able to fill the role of adviser and friend that payment-by-results had made very difficult for H.M.I.s. The National Union of Teachers, in its memorandum to the Bryce Commission in 1894, made it very clear that it preferred the Board's inspectors to H.M.I.s.

Experience has shown that, whereas the school boards, when appointing advisory inspectors as their eyes and ears in the schools have almost invariably chosen men experienced in the difficulties of the work, and practised in the art of teaching, my Lords of the Education Department have almost invariably appointed as Her Majesty's Inspectors of Schools men who lack such experience and practice. And whilst the work of inspectors appointed by school boards has been generally helpful to the schools the work of many of the inspectors appointed by the Education Department has, to a very serious extent, been harmful to the schools.

How far this is to be taken at its face value, how far

it reflects the insurmountable barrier set up between H.M.I.s and teachers by payment-by-results and how far it is influenced by class prejudice must be matters for speculation. There must have been many who thought that it was only a matter of time before the national inspectorate disappeared and the School Boards—and *a fortiori*, the Local Education Authorities after 1902—became responsible for the inspection of their own schools. Why this did not happen will be considered in the next section.

Since, from 1870 onwards, religious instruction in church schools was not inspected by H.M.I.s, the Churches had either to abandon the regular inspection of religious teaching in their schools or appoint inspectors of their own. Broadly speaking the Free Churches and the Roman Catholic Church adopted the former course and the Anglicans the latter. Some vestige of inspection of Free Church schools lasted until 1901 and of Roman Catholic schools until 1884, but the Church of England still retains its Diocesan Inspectorate. Little information is available about the first diocesan inspectors after 1870 but one, the Rev. M. C. F. Morris (Morris, 1922) who was inspector in the York diocese from 1874 to 1879, has left an interesting and amusing account of his experiences to which reference is made in the bibliography.

1898-1944

The story of H.M. Inspectorate in the forty-six years between the abandonment of payment-by-results and the 1944 Act, is mainly one of expansion. The century began with re-organization. The elementary inspectorate formed a separate branch under its own Chief Inspector, Mr (afterwards Sir) Cyril Jackson. It included four different ranks—H.M. Inspectors; the new rank of Junior Inspector, recruited from young men with a University background but not always with teaching experience; women inspectors, who were accorded the rank of H.M.I. but who formed a separate corps under their own Chief Woman Inspector; and Assistant Inspectors, who remained, as before, a sort of N.C.O. branch, though they were now allowed the courtesy of 'Esq' (Boothroyd, 1923, 26). The secondary inspectorate was established in 1904 with Mr W. C. Fletcher, Headmaster of Liverpool College, as its Chief and with a nucleus of the South Kensington Inspectorate as his staff, and, at the same time, a Technological Inspectorate under Mr C. A. Buckmaster took the place of the South Kensington body. This tripartite organization survived until 1944.

The first task of the elementary branch was to try to remove the effects of thirty-six years of payment-by-results. The *Instructions* issued in 1898 state that:

> Inspection should not include any of the processes heretofore employed in formal examination. The inspection of a school, so far as it relates to the instruction given, consists chiefly in the observation of methods pursued by the teacher; and any questioning that may be employed should be confined to the purpose of ascertaining how far these methods have been successful.

Inspectors had to go back to where their predecessors had been in 1862, to live down their sad reputation and change their habits. It was largely the pressure of inspectorial opinion which had led to the decision to abolish the results system, but changes came slowly, and it was many years before teachers lost their fear of the inspector's visit. The structure of the inspectorate, with H.M.I.s who were mainly public school and Oxbridge products without any experience of elementary teaching, and Assistant Inspectors, who knew the elementary schools from first-hand experience, but of whom many were men of limited education, may strike us now as curious and perhaps indefensible. There was, in fact, much to be said for it. It was, at the time, the only means by which a broad educational outlook could be combined with the skill and experience of practitioners who had themselves been elementary teachers, to influence popular education. As time went on, the quality and qualifications of the Assistant Inspectors improved and an increasing, though limited, number of them were promoted to H.M.I. When in 1944, the Assistant Inspector grade was abolished, there were very few Assistant Inspectors about whose promotion to H.M.I. qualms were felt, and H.M.I.s almost unanimously welcomed the change.

The class structure of the inspectorate became an issue in 1910. Sir Cyril Jackson had been succeeded as Chief Inspector of Elementary Schools by Mr E. G. A. Holmes, who circulated to inspectors a confidential document concerning recruitment to the inspectorate, which contained the following rash words:

As compared with the ex-elementary teacher usually engaged in the hopeless task of surveying, or trying to survey, a wide field of action from a well-worn groove, the inspector of the public school and university type has the advantage of being able to look at elementary education from a point of view of complete detachment and therefore of being able to handle its problems with freshness and originality (Holmes, 1910).

This was a perfectly defensible statement but it was

not a wise one. The contents of the circular leaked out and there was a tremendous row, of which one of the worst consequences was the removal from the position of Permanent Secretary of Sir Robert Morant, probably the most able man who has ever held the post. Otherwise, not very much came of it. As we have seen, the two grades continued until 1944 and, though an attempt was made to broaden the social background from which H.M.I.s were recruited, the higher ranks in the Elementary Inspectorate continued to be largely of the Oxford and Cambridge type. This was even more marked in the Secondary, though not in the Technological, branch.

The first positive innovation which marked the change in attitude that followed the abandonment of payment-by-results was the appearance in 1905 of the *Handbook of Suggestions for the Consideration of Teachers*. The Handbook was re-issued in 1909, 1918, 1926 and 1937, each edition reflecting changes in outlook and emphasis, but from the beginning strong emphasis was laid on the freedom and responsibility of the teacher. The preface to the first edition contained the following words, which indicate how quickly the Department (it had become the Board of Education in 1903) had moved in seven years:

Neither the present volume nor any development or amendments of it are designed to impose any regulations supplementary to those contained in the Code. The only uniformity of practice that the Board of Education desire to see in the teaching of Public Elementary Schools is that each teacher shall think for himself, and work out for himself such methods of teaching as may use his powers to the best advantage and be best suited to the particular needs and conditions of the school. Uniformity in details of practice (except in the mere routine of school management) is not desirable even if it were attainable. But freedom implies a corresponding responsibility in its use. However, the teacher need not let the sense of his responsibility depress him or make him afraid to be his natural self in school. Children are instinctively attracted by sincerity and cheerfulness; and the greatest teachers have been thoroughly human in their weaknesses as well as in their strength.

The joint authors of all the handbooks were the inspectors, and if these words, which might have been written yesterday, did not reflect the outlook and attitude of every individual H.M.I. fifty years ago, they did represent the official policy of the inspectorate.

In the twenties and thirties the Board published numbers of educational pamphlets, written by inspectors and dealing with various aspects of education and subjects such as music and crafts; and residential courses for elementary teachers began to be organized, though it was not until the mid-thirties that anything much was done for teachers of the primary age-groups. Here again it was the inspectors who directed and staffed the courses and who became increasingly the spearhead of educational advance.

The majority of teachers were still rather timid and fearful of experiment. More than one inspector in the thirties had the experience, when he had recommended some innovation or unorthodoxy, of being greeted with the question: 'You may say this, Mr X, but what will happen to me if some other H.M.I. doesn't like it?' Gradually, however, as the fears proved groundless and new blood came into the profession, the situation improved, and by 1944 a civilized, professional relationship was beginning to be firmly established between H.M.I.s and teachers.

To return to the beginning of the century, the upholding

of the Cockerton Judgement in 1901 led to the Balfour Act of 1902, and the establishment of county and municipal secondary schools, all of them of the grammar-school type. The Secondary Inspectorate, formed in 1904, had the task of helping these new schools to take shape, as well as of inspecting the existing endowed schools. Schools not in receipt of grant could apply for inspection but had to pay for it. An increasing number of independent schools did this and it was the Secondary branch which was responsible for inspecting not only the public schools but also the preparatory schools that fed them.

The instrument which this new branch created for inspecting Secondary Schools was the Full Inspection. A team of inspectors, sufficient in numbers and varied qualifications to do justice to each particular school and, necessarily, coming from a wide area, would spend from Tuesday to Friday morning looking at every aspect of the work in the school, discussing it with the teachers and, after a lengthy meeting among themselves on the Thursday evening, would each meet the head teacher on the Friday and give him or her an account of their findings. One member of the team known as the Reporting Inspector (R.I.), who was usually the inspector in whose district the school lay, and who would have paid at least one preliminary visit, had the job of meeting the governors on the Friday afternoon and of co-ordinating his colleagues' reports into a whole. The Report was printed, and, some weeks later issued to the school.

This intensive inspection, which is still in its essentials practised, though very much less frequently than formerly, was a considerable ordeal for head teacher and staff. The early secondary inspectors were men of high academic qualifications, but it took a little time for this largely inexperienced body to get on easy terms with the raw new schools in their bright new buildings, and with the staff who worked in them. Probably most of the teachers found the ordeal less alarming and more useful than they had expected, and the best teachers got the most from it.

When the inspectors were not taking part in F.I.s they would be in their own districts and would pay informal visits to their own secondary schools. Long before the Elementary Branch began to organize teachers' courses, the Secondary Inspectors ran courses for teachers of various subjects in secondary schools. They wrote most of the early pamphlets, and some were sent on visits abroad and wrote accounts of what they had seen. They played a major part in the formation of grammar-school education and in bringing the independent secondary schools into touch with new developments. In 1944, when they disappeared as a separate branch, they had a distinguished record behind them.

The technological branch of the inspectorate was released in 1904 from the hybrid duties imposed upon it in 1898, but it remained throughout its existence responsible for an extraordinary variety of subjects and institutions. The inspectors began by turning their attention to Evening Continuation Schools and by encouraging group courses which included several correlated subjects, as distinct from courses in isolated subjects. Full-time courses in technical schools, day classes for apprentices and day continuation classes all developed, largely as a result of the inspectors' influence. It must be remembered that until 1944 further education was not a 'duty' imposed on L.E.A.s, but a 'power' which they could exercise if they chose. Few, if any, employed any advisory staff for F.E. and only H.M. Inspectors had the knowledge and experience which the

L.E.A.s needed. Their influence was therefore potentially very great but depended partly at least upon their powers of persuasion. From 1908 to 1918 they made comprehensive surveys of the provision for, and needs of further education in every part of the country, foreshadowing in this the idea of 'procedure by Scheme' laid down in the Education Act of 1918. As time went on, their numbers were strengthened by experts in different technologies and with industrial and commercial experience. They recruited women for the inspection of domestic and trade subjects for girls, while the expansion of classes under the auspices of the Workers' Educational Association and the University Extra-Mural Boards necessitated the appointment of inspectors with literary, historical and economic qualifications, who sometimes seemed a little out of place in a branch in which engineers, builders, mining experts and the like predominated.

The institution of National Certificates, as the joint concerns of Professional Bodies, Technical Institutions and the Department, enormously increased the responsibilities and the powers of H.M. Inspectors, who had not only to approve the courses proposed by the individual technical colleges, but also to decide which colleges were suitably staffed and equipped to hold particular courses. They had to maintain contacts with industry and commerce and keep up their knowledge of industry's requirements and of labour conditions by visits to factories, mines and offices. Whereas the other two branches lived and worked almost entirely in the world of education, the T. branch, as it was always called in the inspectorate, moved in a much wider sphere. Nor was there ever much danger of their incurring the stigma of 'upper classness' to which, as we have seen, H.M.I.s of other branches were exposed.

It should now be clear why H.M. Inspectorate never gave way to a purely local inspectorate such as the N.U.T. had hoped for in 1894. While it might have been possible for the School Boards and L.E.A.s to undertake the inspection of their own elementary schools, as was indeed the case in the L.C.C. schools from 1926 to 1944, it would have been manifestly impossible for any L.E.A. to maintain a staff adequate for the inspection of secondary schools and, even more, technical institutions. Only a national inspectorate could do this economically and effectively. Quite apart from this, the local inspector has two grave disadvantages from the teacher's point of view, however excellent his personal qualities and professional skill. He, or she, shares an employer with the teacher, and is frequently called upon to advise that employer on matters of promotion, possessing thus a power which is quite alien from the complete political and professional detachment of H.M.I.s. Secondly the local inspector is local. Not only is he without the whole network of contacts and information available to H.M. Inspectors but he is too often a fixture, whereas H.M.I.s are moved every ten years or so. This is not to disparage either the quality or the usefulness of the local inspectorates. No H.M.I. who has worked with them, usually in harmony and mutual regard, would wish to do that. The Plowden Council, who looked into the matter, thought that both kinds of inspectorates performed useful and complementary functions and that generally there was too little inspection rather than too much (Plowden, 1967, 941-7). We shall have to take another look at this in Chapter 4.

The philosophy, functions and purposes of H.M. Inspectorate as it now is will be the subject of a later chapter. In this final historical section my concern is principally with its organization. The various changes and modifications that were made in the first hundred years of its existence were only mentioned to the extent that they threw light on its evolution. Its present organization, however, is of importance to all who come within its purview, that is the whole spectrum of English education apart from the Universities. The Youth Services, Community Centres and Services education were added to its responsibilities during the war; the short-term residential colleges and education in prisons and Borstals shortly after; and all independent schools containing more than five children of school age in the 1944 Act. Quite apart from these additions, the re-organization of schools that took place at the time of that Act made the old tripartite organization inappropriate.

That organization was less simple than it appeared. Elementary Inspectors of A.I. rank had to help on so many evenings in the year with the inspection of evening schools, though these were the responsibility of T. Branch. Secondary Inspectors, as we have seen, were responsible for the inspection of preparatory schools, though these were mainly primary in their age range. Full-range elementary schools (5-14) and senior elementary schools (11-14) were entirely outside the field of the Secondary Inspectors. The T. Inspectorate covered adult education and art colleges but not colleges of music. Besides these anomalies, there were numbers of Staff Inspectors, with responsibilities for particular subjects, who cut across all the boundaries. An art specialist, for instance, would visit elementary and secondary schools as well as the art colleges and colleges of education in his area, and it was always possible, though not common, for one branch to borrow from another when some particular need could be met only in this way. Each of the ten territorial divisions was presided over by a single Divisional Inspector who might be drawn from any of the three branches, and, finally, women inspectors, though employed in all three branches, still formed a partially separate corps under a chief who was now designated Senior Woman Inspector.

In 1944 the inspectorate was unified. The rank of A.I. was abolished. Over a short space of time all the remaining A.I.s were promoted, and women, apart from the diminishing and now defunct salary differentiation, were treated in every respect as on a par with men.

The main body of the inspectorate is distributed in appropriate densities over the whole country and is organized in ten divisions. Except for the rarer and more esoteric requirements, the staff of each division is supposed to be able to meet most of the inspection needs of that division, though divisions are not watertight compartments, and for some purposes are grouped in threes. A division is itself divided into districts, each with its own district inspector for primary and secondary schools, with another for further education. An inspector may be in charge of more than one district and most inspectors work in more than one. It is possible for an inspector to be in charge of one district and to work in another under a district inspector who may himself work under him in his own district. A district inspector is no more than *primus inter pares* among his colleagues. His importance is that he is a link between the Department and the Local Education Authority. Every authority thus has two inspectors whom it can properly regard as its own, one for schools and the other for further education, no matter how many others may work regularly or occasionally in its schools.

Similarly every school, every educational institution, has one inspector, known as the General Inspector, who is assigned to it, and no other inspector will visit it without the agreement, general or particular, of the General Inspector. Informal routine inspection may be by one, or more than one, individual but will be arranged privately, without reference to anyone else. For a small school a formal, reporting inspection may be arranged in the same way, but where a larger team is needed, involving borrowings from other districts, the Divisional Inspector will generally come into the picture. Inspectors travel out of their divisions only with the permission of the D.I., or for responsibilities and engagements, e.g. courses, panel meetings etc., which have been centrally arranged with the D.I.s concurrence.

This is the basic organization of inspection. The ten Divisional Inspectors are senior men and women, and they have an overall responsibility for all the inspection that goes on in their territory and for placing and training newcomers. They also have a pastoral responsibility towards all inspectors in their divisions. It is their business to know them with their strengths and weaknesses, cherish them and, on rare occasions, admonish them. This is an important function, because most inspectors have been accustomed, before joining, to the close-knit organization of a school staff and do not always find it easy to adapt themselves to the much looser organization and sometimes solitary work of the inspectorate.

Staff Inspectors have the same status and salary as Divisional Inspectors and there is occasional interchange between the posts. There are fifty-five of them. They too are dispersed over the whole country with some concentration in the London area, and they are specialists either in a subject or in some phase or aspect of education (e.g. comprehensive schools, nursery education, special educational treatment). They are advisers and consultants to the Secretary of State and to their colleagues and they keep in touch not only with the schools and colleges but also with the appropriate organizations which share their concerns (e.g. the Staff Inspector for drama would be in contact with the British Drama League, the B.B.C., the R.A.D.A., etc.). Most Staff Inspectors have a national coverage and have a right of entry everywhere, though they would not normally visit a school or college without the knowledge of the General Inspector.

The 'high command' consists of the Senior Chief Inspector and the six Chief Inspectors. The way in which responsibilities are shared out among the Chief Inspectors is not fixed, but generally three are concerned with schools, two with further education and one with training. All have their headquarters at Curzon Street and they act as the Department's chief educational advisers and as the heads of the branches of inspection for which they are responsible. They make regular field visits to all the ten divisions and as many others, including, of course, visits to schools, colleges, clubs, etc. as they can find time.

This organizational structure is intended to produce flexibility and the maximum use of talents. It is served by a network of communications, in the form of Divisional and Phase (e.g. primary) Conferences, panel meetings (e.g. music and engineering) and working parties, and by a limited flow of memoranda and information, so that all inspectors are kept informed about what is going on generally and in their own fields of interest, and the Chief and Staff Inspectors kept in touch. To keep this information service efficient and to avoid swamping the inspectorate with paper is an aim kept under constant review by Chief Inspectors and Divisional Inspectors, who meet for two days in London five times a year for this and other purposes.

3

The inspectorate today

Recruitment and appointment

Until 1926, H.M. Inspectors were recruited by patronage.
Anyone who wished to become an H.M.I. had to find the
right person to back him. The Board of Education was the
last public department to abandon this once universal
method of choosing civil servants of the higher ranks. It
may have been some lingering recollection of this which
led to the suspicions voiced by a teachers' delegation that
visited the Ministry some ten years ago. They wished to
be assured that there were no back doors into H.M.
Inspectorate, that the periodic advertisements were what
they appeared to be and that everyone who was appointed
to the inspectorate had to go through an identical process.

The representatives of the Office and the Inspectorate
who received the delegation were able to give them the
assurance that they asked for. Every candidate must complete the same application form. A general advertisement,
i.e. one without any specifying of special requirements,
usually results in something a little under 1,000 applications. A considerable proportion of these can be rejected
on sight. They come from candidates who are too old,
too young, too inexperienced, completely unqualified or
whose qualifications are not what are currently wanted.

The Inspectorate may, for instance, require a linguist with a special knowledge of Spanish. An applicant with firsts in French and German will not do, though he may be told that if he applies again in two years' time the Department will be interested in his application. There may remain, after this preliminary sifting, 500 or so applications. These are referred to any inspector who knows the applicant professionally and to the staff inspector most immediately interested. If their comment is favourable, the professional references are then taken up and the survivors of these successive siftings are interviewed.

The interviewing board is presided over by one of the Civil Service Commissioners. It is normally attended by the S.C.I., one of the C.I.s, any S.I. immediately interested and a member of the Establishment branch. The interview, which lasts about forty-five minutes, is conducted with the maximum of informality, each member of the board being free to take part and to question or converse with the applicant in any way that he thinks is likely to reveal the qualities and interests that are being sought. What these are will be discussed in the following section.

When all the applicants have been interviewed, a process that may take many days spread over a period of weeks, the final list is made and the character references are taken up. Provided that nothing then comes to light which might raise doubts about the suitability of any of the applicants (it almost never does), offers are dispatched. If all these are accepted the process is complete, apart from some requirements of the Civil Service Commission concerning health and so on. If there are any refusals, offers may be made to second choices.

Soon after an offer has been accepted the recruit will be told in what Division he is to serve, and will be put in touch with the Divisional Inspector, who will tell him in what area of the Division he should look for a headquarters. In this a good deal of latitude is allowed, but the headquarters must be in a place which allows an economical use of time. An inspector who was to work in Manchester might be allowed to live in Knutsford or Alderley Edge, but he could not live in Chester or, if very exceptionally he were allowed to, he could not claim any expenses for the journey between the two towns or for subsistence when he was obliged to spend the night or a long day in Manchester. Furthermore he would have to satisfy the Divisional Inspector that he could and would spend as much working time in Manchester as if he lived there.

Each new inspector is on probation for a period of two years and is put under the immediate care and guidance of an experienced colleague whom it has recently become fashionable to call his 'mentor'. The probation is by no means a nominal one. The newcomer's bearing and manner in school and elsewhere are carefully noted, and any shortcomings are frankly discussed with him. Only exceptionally do newcomers fail their probation; if, at the end of the first year, failure looks likely, a clear warning is given, so that the inspector may have time to make other plans for himself if his probation is not confirmed twelve months later. If he shows promise he will be given some responsibilities long before his probation ends, but in the first few weeks at least he will usually work in company with his mentor or some other more senior colleague. One of the C.I.s will almost certainly spend a day or two with him during his probation and his D.I. will see as much of him as he can.

It is claimed for this process that it opens the door wide to applicants, that careful sifting eliminates the unsuitable but ensures the consideration of a reasonable number of 'possibles'; that those who are considered are very carefully chosen or rejected, and that the survivors are well-trained for a job that demands a very high quality of manners and sympathy. I think the claim is justified. It is obviously impossible to know how many of the rejected candidates would have been good inspectors if they had been appointed. A number apply again but the original decision is only rarely altered and then only because increased experience and maturity have made the applicant a better choice. The very small numbers eliminated by probation suggest that the selection procedure is at least adequate, and the high public reputation of the inspectorate, which is jealously guarded by opinion within it, supports this conclusion. The system is not perfect, and men and women as they grow older, may develop characteristics which deny the promise they once showed, or may quite simply fail to live up to that promise. Or they may find that some sphere of activity other than inspection attracts them and perhaps return to teaching or transfer to administration. But this is a very small minority, not more than one or two per cent. It is very important that this should be so. An unstable inspectorate would be an inefficient one and an inspectorate in which personal and professional quality was not of high rank would be a disaster.

Qualifications

No attempt has ever been made to lay down with any precision the academic, professional and personal qualifications required in an inspector, and it must be hoped that no reforming politician or tidy-minded official will ever be tempted to try it. The vast range of work required of H.M.

Inspectorate and the variety of educational institutions inspected must be reflected in the variety of inspectorial qualifications. Nursery Schools, primary schools, special schools and secondary schools of all descriptions, technical colleges, adult education colleges, W.E.A. and University extension work, colleges of education, Services education, education in prisons and Borstals, community centres, youth clubs, museum education, art and music colleges, drama and ballet schools, schools for teaching English to foreigners, day-continuation classes—the qualifications for inspecting these cannot be codified. The inspectorate must be able to recruit people with the varied knowledge and experience that the work requires, and must and does look for recruits in all the fields represented. It would be totally impossible, even if it were desirable, so to arrange matters that every inspectorial visit to whatever institution was paid by an expert. There must be experts available, but there must also be, in the inspectorate as a whole, enough versatility, enough width of interest, to make it possible for the majority of inspectors to be effective in wider fields than the one in which each is specially qualified. This does not mean that an historian must be expected to inspect sixth-form physics, or an engineer a class for the partially-sighted, but it does mean that a narrowly specialist outlook is no asset in H.M. Inspectorate. The English education system being what it now is, this requirement may be increasingly difficult to find in the years ahead.

It is not uncommon for resolutions to be put forward at teachers' conferences that schools should be inspected only by inspectors who have themselves had teaching experience in schools of the same kind. It would be impossible to carry on inspection at all if such a condition were laid down. A more reasonable demand is that no one should be appointed to the inspectorate who has not himself been a teacher. For more than fifty years this has been something very near a condition of appointment. There have been very few exceptions—I think, only one in the past twenty years. The likelihood of anyone's being appointed who has had no experience as a teacher is now remote, but the Department's hands should not be tied.

The personal qualifications looked for in an inspector are, if hard to define, obviously of great importance. Anyone who is given the legal right to visit and inspect any school and classroom in England, who has great freedom in the arrangement of his time and who frequently works on his own and nearly always without any supervision, must clearly display high standards of integrity, judgement, manners and humility. In his dealings with the opposite sex and with children he must be above reproach. Though his private life is his own it must not be such as to raise doubts about his behaviour in school. Clearly all that the selectors can do is to obtain such information as they can reasonably ask for, look for signs and back their own judgement. Once the appointment is made, the traditions of the inspectorate must be relied upon to be maintained with enough sensitiveness to distinguish between normally changing customs and undesirable departures from them.

Two personal experiences may at this point be illuminating. Shortly after my appointment I was discussing the work with the S.C.I. (Sir Henry Richards) who said: 'You will have very little power but you may have a lot of influence. The amount of that influence will be in inverse ratio to the extent that you throw your weight about.' Many years later, when I had found out how true that was, I was considering an application from a man of some distinction who had many of the qualities for which we were looking but about whom I felt some half-formed doubts. I wrote to a colleague who knew the applicant better and asked him what he thought. His full and careful reply contained the sentence: 'I am afraid that inspection is too sharp a weapon to put into his hands.' An inspector, national or local, who fails in personal relationships—and this includes being merely negative and nice as well as being overbearing—can do great harm, not only to the confidence established between the inspectorate and the teaching profession, but to the education of the whole area in which he works.

In view of the past history of H.M. Inspectorate, and because of the current sensitiveness to such matters, it may be wondered whether there is not still a hidden, un-acknowledged bias in favour of applicants with public school and Oxbridge antecedents, whether in fact, the Holmes Circular is quite dead. The number of such appli-cants is a very small proportion of the whole and so is the number of appointments. Both proportions are de-creasing. It is true that, in terms of promotion, the tiny public school minority have done very well. Although only two out of the six holders of the Senior Chief Inspector-ship have been educated at public schools, in 1966 four of the six C.I.s and five of the nine men D.I.s were public school men. Among Staff Inspectors the proportion was much smaller. It would be beyond the scope of this book to enquire into the reasons for the declining interest in H.M. Inspectorate shown by the class of which it was once entirely composed, but there can be no doubt that, for a long time, there has been no bias in favour of that class or, conversely, that its members have been able to make a contribution to the body out of all proportion to their numbers.

The Brotherhood

In chapter two I gave some account of the organization of H.M. Inspectorate, and in the following chapter I shall discuss the functions and professional work of that and of local inspectorates. Here I want to say a very little about the internal life of H.M. Inspectorate as I knew it. This is not solely the private affair of its members. To the extent that it is I shall not trespass into it. But the way in which the organization, as a social rather than as a professional group, regards itself and arranges its affairs, has some effect upon its relations with teachers and administrators and may therefore be of interest to readers of this book.

Thirty or forty years ago the Inspectorate was commonly referred to by its members as the Brotherhood. The term is now, apparently, extinct. Oddly enough it has become more and not less appropriate, with the amalgamation of the three branches and the disappearance of the A.I. grade. At no period of its history has its hierarchical structure been overemphasized. Nobody is 'sir', and from the day he joins a man drops the 'Mr'. Women retain the custom of being called 'Miss' or 'Mrs' and calling men 'Mr' but the increasing, indeed almost universal use, of Christian names has made this distinction unimportant. Egalitarianism goes deeper than speech habits. There is no chain of command. It is obviously convenient for the Chief Inspectors, Divisional Inspectors and Staff Inspectors to share out responsibilities, but every H.M.I. can approach the S.C.I. direct; the Chief Inspectors and Staff Inspectors do not, in any sense, command teams; and the authority of the Divisional Inspector is limited. Once a responsibility is given, it is for the individual inspector to carry it out in his own way. This freedom was once greater than it now is. Many educational developments have increased the need for teamwork and for surveys covering wide areas, and the authority of the Divisional Inspector has necessarily been extended, an unavoidable and possibly a regrettable development. Nevertheless individual freedom remains a reality and any encroachment upon it is regarded with suspicion, and generally made with hesitation. How long this will last remains to be seen.

The social division into two ranks disappeared in 1945 but now, as then, there is an enormous variety of social background in H.M. Inspectorate. Class has little or no effect on its internal life, or such was my impression. To check this, I asked a former colleague who came from a completely working-class background what he thought about this. His reply was as follows:

> I think the values the Inspectorate still shows a great respect for, have a large element of snobbery in them— houses in the country, deerstalker hats, Rolls-Royces, Jaguars and other prestige-bringing cars, expertise in wines, silver, old furniture and so on.

He goes on:

> I was impressed from the beginning with the way in which men and women of the most varied background could, without strain or apparent effort, look with imaginative sympathy at the problems of primary and secondary modern schools. Any form of class consciousness would, in my view, have got short shrift at any gathering of inspectors anywhere, but I can honestly say that I have never seen any need for short shrift, or of an admonition or regulator of any kind.

The somewhat paradoxical picture that forms itself from these two comments from the same source is perhaps a true one. The inspectorate has always valued individuality and a modest degree of eccentricity in its members, but this has never in my experience impaired either its professional integrity or its strong corporate sense. To belong to the Brotherhood is, as one inspector once said, to work with the nicest body of people in the world, but it is also to be obliged to conform to a very high standard.

4

The inspectorate at work

The Select Committee's report

In July 1968 was published the report by a Select Committee of the House of Commons on H.M. Inspectorate in England and Wales. With the report was printed all the written, and most of the oral evidence received by the Committee, the latter presented under cross-examination. The evidence came from the administrative side of the Department of Education and Science, from H.M.I.s and local inspectors and from various bodies of teachers and administrators. It provides uniquely interesting material for considering the aims, functions, methods and qualifications of inspectors now and in the future.

The views expressed in the evidence are not only varying, as might be expected, but frequently, and on matters of major importance, diametrically opposed to each other. One highly qualified and distinguished witness for instance, wanted to see a much smaller inspectorate which he described as a *corps d'élite*, a step which some other witnesses, no less well qualified, viewed with the deepest apprehension. There were those who thought that formal inspection should cease and that inspectors should become simply advisers and consultants, and others who felt that advice

45

not based on inspection would be useless. On one matter there was virtual unanimity, namely the merits of H.M. Inspectors. Even those who disliked their functions paid tribute to their qualities and nobody wished to see them disappear altogether, at any rate for some time to come.

The evidence revealed the existence of a good deal of mythology concerning the inspectorate. One Chief Education Officer said 'before the last war, say twenty or thirty years ago, they were still in many cases titled ladies and gentlemen' (Select Committee, 1968, 837). Making every allowance for picturesque exaggeration, this is a fantastic statement. At the time of which he spoke one H.M. Inspector was a baronet and one an Earl's daughter, and between 1839 and 1914 I can find only three Honourables. It is extraordinary how persistent this baseless myth of a mainly aristocratic inspectorate has been.

A rather more serious misconception was shared by almost all the witnesses, and seems to persist in the minds of the Committee itself, namely that the full-dress formal inspection, which is now being largely abandoned has been, until recently, the common practice. It was, as stated in Chapter 3, invented by the new Secondary Inspectorate after 1902 and, until 1944, it was used only for the inspection of grammar schools, public and preparatory schools and institutions of higher education. Even with these it was not the sole kind of inspection, but formal inspections were interspersed with informal visits by general inspectors and specialists. The Elementary Inspectorate never used it at all. They rarely even used the word 'inspection' and never talked about 'full inspections'. They used the terms 'visit' and 'report visit'. The second was often as informal as the first. It rarely involved more than two inspectors and sometimes only one. It was unannounced and the inspector often made up his mind to write a report only at the end of the visit. Even the large new senior elementary schools, which in 1944 changed their names to secondary modern schools, were seldom reported on by a team of more than three inspectors, and the non-reporting visits were more frequent and regarded by the inspectors as equally important and much more enjoyable. It was only in 1944, when H.M. Inspectorate was unified and a frantic effort made to give 'parity of esteem' to all kinds of secondary schools, that the full inspection spread to secondary modern schools and a little later to primary schools. The old elementary districts were almost completely self-contained. When I was District Inspector of elementary schools in Manchester, Salford and the Isle of Man, I never had more than three, and sometimes only two, assistants, and with this staff I had to manage everything, apart from a little help from a handful of specialists in handicraft, homecraft and P.E. (there was none for music), who covered the whole of Lancashire and Cheshire. While there were obvious disadvantages in this arrangement, it did lead to a familiarity and informality in all our visits to schools, whether we were reporting or not. We knew the schools and they knew us and they rarely met an inspector who was not on the District staff. It is this kind of relationship, minus the report, which a good many of the Committee's witnesses seem to be looking for, though, as it appears to me, without always realizing its implications. To these I shall return more than once later in the book.

The inspectorate in its own eyes

Although much was said in the evidence to the Committee and in the Committee's own report about the changing role of the inspectorate, I am confident that if the inspectors who were in post in 1933, when I joined the body, and in 1966 when I left it, could meet together and discuss the job there would prove to be a surprising amount of common ground between them. They would, I think, be unanimous that their first task was to visit schools, and that what they did when they got there must be for each individual to decide. Their first aim would be to look into what was happening, the work being done, the human relationships, the appropriateness and use of the building and equipment, everything in fact, with the further aims of helping the teachers in any way in which they needed help and of satisfying themselves that the children were receiving as good an education as possible. They would not separate in their minds the functions of inspection and advice, consultation and discussion, and would feel that to advise without first of all having inspected, or to set up as consultants without free discussion first, would be intolerably arrogant. Where the two groups would most clearly diverge would be on the matter of written reports.

The older group would all have been trained to regard the written report as a major part of an inspector's duties. They would have been expected to write in faultless English and, because the Assistant Inspectors were not always quite reliable in this respect, they were obliged to submit their reports to their District Inspectors who alone were allowed to sign them. They would have had impressed upon them the necessity for scrupulous accuracy and fairness, for avoiding any statement which, if challenged, they could not substantiate, for remembering that, although the report was nominally to the President of the Board of Education, it would be read by the School Managers, and for including nothing in it which had not already been said, in stronger rather than weaker terms, to the head teacher at the time of the visit. They would have been trained, moreover, to try to visit their schools once a year or once in two years at least, and to write a report once in five, six or seven.

The contemporary group would take a very different view. They would point out that the increase in the size (though not the number) of schools and school population and in the variety of new demands made on inspectors, made frequent reporting impossible and that very infrequent reports were less valuable, if only because of the rapidity with which a report became out-of-date. Also that more could usually be done by informal visiting than by the kind of full inspections which the production of a report usually involved. They would, however, be reluctant, I think, to abandon all reporting and would like to preserve the written report as an inspectorial instrument which might sometimes still be needed, certainly in independent schools and probably in maintained schools. They would all know that cases sometimes arise where a thorough-going investigation of a school by a completely independent person is needed, followed by a written report which all concerned can read, and that where some outstanding work is being done or some especially interesting development is taking place, it should be put on record in an available form, in other words in a report.

The official report is hedged about with a number of regulations, the most important of which is that, although it is confidential it is not secret. It ensures at once that inspectors can write frankly and that those about whom they write know what has been said about them. No other information about a teacher is supposed to be given by an inspector to the Department or to the Local Education

49

Authority. The only exceptions are where a Local Authority recommends the extension or determination of probation, and cases of misconduct reported by the Authority
to the D.E.S. In both these cases H.M.I. will be asked for
his comments. If the report is to disappear altogether this
safeguard disappears with it, and all sorts of information
about schools and teachers, much of it laudatory no doubt
but some at least adverse, will be passed on by inspectors
in secret. This aspect of the matter was scarcely mentioned
in the evidence to the Committee. If inspectors became
simply advisers and disseminators as well as informants
to the Department it would be naïve to suppose that what
they said and wrote would never reflect upon individual
schools and teachers. This issue will have to be resolved
whatever happens, and I think the inspectors themselves
will be the first to insist upon this.

Inspectors regard themselves as first and foremost the
colleagues of the teachers they visit, whose usefulness
depends upon the width and diversity of their experience.
Although they often hanker after teaching, they would not
agree that, after some years in the inspectorate, they get
out of touch or out of date. Many witnesses seemed to
think that this was likely to happen and recommended
periods of return to teaching or, in one instance, the end-
ing of inspection as a career so that it became simply a
secondment (Select Committee, 1968, 1,092). The desira-
bility of this can, I think, be exaggerated. Nearly all inspectors would feel that their experience has kept them much
more up to date and much more in touch than many of the
teachers they visit. Moreover they act as teachers whenever
they run courses, usually with success. Provided that their
numbers and organization allow them to spend a substantial
part of their time in the classroom they are not likely to

become remote or 'viewy'. Nevertheless inspectors have for long been conscious of the difficulty of keeping up to date with all the developments in their own subjects let alone in others. In 1967, the Department agreed to the holding of refresher courses for inspectors, and in 1968 the first of these was held. It was followed, before the end of the year, by six others, and more were planned for 1969 and 1970. A very wide range of subjects has been covered, including various aspects of educational technology. This is an innovation welcome to inspectors and when the sabbatical year for which they have longed is granted (if it ever is) they will have little of which to complain.

Whether this picture of inspectors through their own eyes corresponds to what other people think of them, and whether changing conditions will make it possible for them to go on in this way, will be discussed in later sections. Inspectors themselves still have no doubt that their place is in school.

Inspectors and the Department

The relationship of H.M. Inspectorate to the Department of Education and Science is of great importance in the English system, and it has been confused by another piece of mythology which has infected inspectors themselves, the mythology of being 'Her Majesty's'. When the inspectorate was established in 1839 there was no department of education and they were chosen, as we have seen, by the Home Secretary and were responsible to a committee of the Privy Council. The only constitutional way of appointing them was by an act of the Sovereign in Council, and so by an historical accident, they became 'Her Majesty's

Inspectors'. They are, however, employed by the Department, like any other civil servant who works for it, and the survival of the original method of appointment confers no independence upon them. Some inspectors in the past have deluded themselves that it did and nearly all inspectors have been proud of the title. As the Permanent Under-Secretary said to the Committee: 'It delights the people who enjoy it' (Select Committee, 1968, 55). The belief that being 'H.M.' conferred a special independence on H.M. Inspectors was not confined to inspectors and was shared by many administrators and teachers. But if the cause was a myth, the independence was not. The independence is genuine and important, but it is not unlimited, and its extent and nature require a brief consideration.

The organization of the inspectorate under an S.C.I. who ranks just below Deputy Secretary and who, if the Committee's recommendation is adopted (Select Committee Report, 1968, B7), will in future have full Deputy Secretary rank, makes for some degree of independence. No one in the office tells an inspector to do something. In day-to-day matters he asks him, and if anything out of the ordinary is required it will be handled by the S.C.I. or one of the Chief Inspectors. The inspectorate serves the office but is not at its beck and call. There is no written constitution in this matter and precisely how it operates has probably varied from time to time, depending to some extent upon the personalities of the heads of the office and the heads of the inspectorate at any given time. A powerful personality like the late Sir Henry Richards who, when S.C.I., was consulted by the Minister about the appointment of the next Permanent Secretary, probably insisted on a degree of independence which his successors would not have thought necessary, and conversely, convinced the office that too much independence was intolerable!

This sort of independence is not, however, the most important kind enjoyed by H.M.I.s, though it has a bearing upon it. An inspector's essential independence is professional. In all educational matters he is free to hold and to express his own opinions, and no departmental control can be exercised upon them. This means that what he says to a teacher or writes in a report is what he really thinks, and is not in any way trimmed to suit government or departmental policy. This independence is safeguarded by the precedent established in the House of Commons in 1863, already described in chapter 2.

There is clearly an area of operation in which the degree of inspectorial independence must be a matter of doubt. This is the area of broad educational policy, and is that in which H.M. Inspectors are dealing with Local Education Authorities, rather than with individual schools and teachers. The Department could not tolerate a situation in which one of its employees was openly and explicitly hostile to a policy which it was implementing at the behest of Parliament. At the same time an inspector is not expected to preach any particular doctrine. That is the job of politicians, not of civil servants. If, in some highly controversial issues such as the suppression of independent schools or of Church schools or of religious instruction, his conscience did not allow him to have any part, he would have to resign, but such sharp divisions as these have, in recent years, been fortunately rare in English education.

It is in this relation of mixed dependence and independence that H.M. Inspectorate stands with the Department. The functions that it fulfils fall into two categories, though the borderline between them is not clear-cut. First it supplies the Department with information and advice. The form in which information was chiefly conveyed in the past, the official report, is, as we have seen, dying and is being replaced by one much less clearly defined and controlled. The information is often requested by the Department; H.M. Inspector is expected to know the answers to questions put to him or to be able to find them out quickly. The questions may be particular, e.g. 'Can you tell us, please, what are the Local Education Authority's intentions with regard to the amalgamation of these two schools?', or general, e.g. 'Could the Inspectorate let us have a list of schools in which teacher-parent relations are especially good?'. It sometimes happens that a question is put to H.M.I.s which could equally well have been answered by a direct approach to the Local Education Authority, but, where comments as well as facts are required, it is obviously convenient for the Department to have on the spot a responsible officer who knows the facts at first hand, and is able to take a detached view of them and assess them crisply and unambiguously.

Information is often volunteered by H.M. Inspector. He is not there simply to answer questions but also to ensure that the Department is kept informed of anything that, in his opinion, it ought to know. The information may be sent direct to the inspector's opposite number at the office or through the Divisional Inspector, Chief Inspector or Staff Inspector. No channel of communication is laid down. H.M. Inspector can choose the one that he thinks appropriate to the circumstances. If the information is of a purely educational kind he will generally use the Staff, or Chief Inspector; if it is administrative, the office. Anything which is of general interest beyond his district will go through the Divisional. It became clear, in the evidence to the Committee, that this rather free-and-easy way of doing things struck the representatives of the Department as 'primitive' (Select Committee, 1968, 122), though the Department may well be as much to blame as the inspectorate in the matter. It is for argument whether a more streamlined, systematic handling of information would be more efficient, and no doubt the joint planning committee recently established in the Department will argue it out.

The advisory functions of the inspectorate *vis-à-vis* the office are closely connected with the informative ones. An inspector will frequently include in his minute of information and comment a recommendation as to what 'we' ought to do. This is expected of him and, if it were omitted, would be asked for. The advice is not always taken. It is the responsibility of the office, not of the inspectorate, to decide upon the course of action, but the inspectors' views are always carefully considered and, in the majority of cases, acted upon.

At headquarters the procedure is a little different, because here, there is a continuing close personal contact between the political, administrative and inspectorial heads. There are standing committees, *ad hoc* committees and frequent meetings formal and informal. At such meetings everybody is free to join in, regardless of his precise function. All behave as equals and policy is thrashed out with everybody making his contribution. Just how this works varies somewhat with the personalities involved. Some ministers, for example, like to have more personal contact with inspectors than others, and some Under-Secretaries work more closely with their corresponding Chief Inspectors than others. This too is doubtless engaging the attention of the joint planning committee.

The second function of the inspectorate *vis-à-vis* the

55

Department was described by more than one witness as diplomatic or ambassadorial. No other government department has at its disposal a similar corps, dispersed throughout the country and in close and frequent contact with the units of local government with which it is concerned. It is the business of a District Inspector to keep in close touch with the Chief Education Officer, with whom he is generally on good personal terms and not infrequently terms of friendship. He will find himself sometimes explaining or expounding, sometimes defending, the Department's policies, discussing their implications in local conditions, communicating information which has not yet reached the paper stage, and, at the same time, discovering more about the authority's difficulties, hopes and intentions and, sometimes, defending the authority to the Department. Such a relationship demands great tact, judgement and integrity. There is an element in it of being jack-of-both-sides and, though H.M.I. must never be in the pocket of the Chief Education Officer, he must always try to understand the Chief Education Officer's point of view and interpret it with the right mixture of sympathy and objectivity to the Department.

It would be surprising if the relationship and the functions just described never led to tension between the Department and the inspectorate. Some tension must always exist between a headquarters and its field force. The former will tend to regard the latter as dangerously individualistic, partisan and irresponsible. The field force will look on headquarters as timid, bound by red-tape and indifferent to real issues. Now and again this tension, in individual instances, reaches a mildly critical point, but it would be a great mistake, in my opinion, to try to eliminate it. This could only be done, if it could be done at all, by making the inspectorate completely subservient to the office, a relationship of sterility. It is far better to preserve the existing relationship, which allows the difference in approach and outlook to be stimulating and fruitful.

The inspectorate and Local Education Authorities

When I was appointed District Inspector of Manchester at the age of thirty-two, a senior colleague, himself a Mancunian, looked at me closely and said: 'It's a big job for a young man. You'd better watch your step, and don't have a row with the Local Education Authority unless you're very sure of yourself. Remember you can be moved and they can't, and if you are you won't go in a blaze of glory either.' This was very good advice. It is the business of a District Inspector to get on with the Chief Education Officer and, if he is going to condemn an authority's policy, as happened in one area just before the war, he had better be very sure that the Department is behind him. A major set-to between Department and Authority is something that neither side initiates lightly, and an aggressive or contentious District Inspector is more likely to make trouble for himself than for anybody else.

The relationship between H.M.I. and Local Education Authority is the counterpart of that between H.M.I. and Department. He must represent the Department with firmness and dignity, he must preserve his professional independence, and he must show understanding of the Authority's position without automatically underwriting it. The Authority does not want a policeman breathing down its neck; nor does it want a 'yes' man. A powerful Authority would not tolerate petty interference or fussiness, nor would it respect anyone incapable of taking an independent

57

line. The District Inspector, man or woman, must be a personality, with a mind above status and comparative salaries and other such trivialities, able to hold his or her own, modestly but steadily, in any company. It is because the inspectorate has, on the whole, been able to appoint such people to District Inspector posts that the peculiar triangular relationship has worked. All the Local Education Authority witnesses before the Committee agreed that the District Inspector was a valuable, if not indispensable component in the administrative complex (Select Committee, 1968, 356-439, 629-56, 827-71).

It is perhaps more surprising that the representatives of the local inspectors and organizers, i.e. those appointed by Local Education Authorities, took the same favourable view (Select Committee, 1968, 657-730). Here there might well be a clash of interests, and the much greater prestige of H.M. Inspectors, to which the teachers' representatives made specific reference, might be expected to arouse feelings of envy if not resentment among their local colleagues.

That this seldom happens must be attributed partly to the good personal relations generally existing between H.M. Inspectors and their local counterparts. They regard each other as colleagues and allies and often as friends. Although their functions overlap, especially in large areas such as London and Manchester, they differ much more. The staffing of schools, the placing and transfer of teachers, the supervision of newly appointed teachers, promotion to posts of responsibility and headships, and, save in cases of doubt, the certifying of probation are all exclusively the concern of the local inspectors. Courses for teachers on a local level are their responsibility, though H.M.I. can, and usually does, help with them. Many local inspectors are not really inspectors at all but organizers. Their job is to stimulate and develop some particular subject or activity —art, music, P.E., homecraft, youth activities, etc. They are more like peripatetic teachers than inspectors. Furthermore many authorities do not employ them at all. When the Plowden Council made enquiries in 1964, they found that only fifty Local Education Authorities out of 162 in England and Wales, employed inspectors or organizers, other than for Youth (Plowden, 1967, 947), and although this number has probably increased in the past few years, there is nothing remotely like a national coverage.

The Select Committee naturally paid a lot of attention to the fact of the existence of the two inspectorates and to the possibility of securing closer integration or even amalgamation, with its obvious economic advantages. The Maud Report is now available but the Government's intentions with regard to it are not. If there are to be fewer and larger local authorities the arrangements for the inspection of schools will clearly be affected and it may be that some of the work now done by H.M. Inspectorate will be undertaken by mixed teams of H.M. Inspectors, L.E.A. inspectors and perhaps teachers. There is clearly room for experiment here and I hope the opportunity will be taken, always provided that the independence of the teams is safeguarded, a point to which I shall return in the final chapter.

Inspectors and teachers

H.M. Inspectors would hold that they stand or fall by their usefulness to teachers, and that this usefulness depends absolutely upon their getting into the schools, looking at the children's activities and productions and discussing these with them and their teachers. It will be interesting to see how they and their task look to teachers, and here the

59

evidence supplied to the Select Committee is of unique importance. Never before has such a representative body of evidence been available.

The teachers' organizations which gave oral evidence to the Committee were as follows: the National Union of Teachers (membership open to all teachers), the National Association of Schoolmasters (membership limited to men teachers), the Incorporated Association of Preparatory Schools (boys' preparatory schools recognized as efficient), the Headmasters' Conference (boys' public schools), the Joint Four (the Association of Head Masters, the association of Head Mistresses), the Association of Assistant Masters, the Association of Assistant Mistresses—all secondary school bodies with a strong grammar school bias—and the Association of Teachers in Technical Institutions. Mr Michael Duane, formerly Headmaster of Risinghill School, was interviewed as an individual. In addition the following teachers' organizations submitted memoranda: Association of Headmistresses of Preparatory Schools (girls' preparatory schools), the Association of Head Mistresses of recognized Independent Schools, Association of Teachers of Maladjusted children, Catholic Teachers' Federation and the National College of the Teachers of the Deaf. As has already been stated all the evidence was, in general, favourable to the inspectorate, but it will be instructive to look a little more closely at what was said, either in writing or orally, by some of the organizations listed above.

The National Union of Teachers felt that the independence of H.M. Inspector was a guarantee of there being no control of the curriculum by the central government (N.U.T. Memo, 1968,14). They viewed the establishment of a *corps d'élite*, as recommended by Sir William Alexander (Select Committee, 1968, 258-9), with 'the deepest apprehension since it would diminish the wide and frequent contact between inspector and teacher' (N.U.T. Memo, 1968, 22). They made three very positive suggestions: first, that the full inspection should be abolished, secondly that H.M. Inspectors should be 'on call', available to teachers when invited as well as visiting schools on their own initiative (N.U.T. Memo, 1968, 11), and thirdly that Local Education Authorities should be inspected by H.M. Inspector (N.U.T. Memo, 1968, 7). The first of these, as we have seen, is well on the road to coming about. The second would be only an extension of something that has always been permissible and has sometimes happened. Whether Local Education Authorities would like being subjected to a full inspection just when schools are being freed from it is doubtful. It would be an assault on their freedom which would be much resented and of very dubious value. It would be better to allow H.M. Inspectors to work through influence on backward or recalcitrant authorities, just as they do on schools, rather than arm them with new powers which they certainly do not want.

The National Association of Schoolmasters was the least friendly of the professional bodies. They included in their evidence one or two examples of bad inspectorial behaviour though they went on to emphasize that these were very exceptional (Select Committee, 1968, 908-10). Their main point was to try to draw an uncrossable line between inspection and advice. The former they abominated and wished to see disappear. Even the latter should be restricted, for they stated that 'advice to individual teachers had little value' (N.A.S. Memo, 1968, 13). They seemed to envisage a corps of educational missionaries who seldom penetrated much beyond the headmaster's room and spread doctrine which they had previously evaluated (N.A.S. Memo, 1968,

18-19). This would, of course, completely reverse the role at present filled by H.M. Inspector who begins by going into school, evaluates what he finds and bases his advice upon the evaluation. It was quite surprising to find one of the N.A.S. witnesses commenting: 'They are doing their job extremely well' (Select Committee, 1968, 910). I must here express a strong personal doubt as to whether teachers want to be advised by people who have had no opportunity of seeing what they, or any other teachers presumably, have been doing.

The Headmasters' Conference may be taken as representative of the most powerful and prestigious independent schools and it is interesting that they spoke in very warm terms of appreciation of H.M. Inspector and, in contrast to the National Union of Teachers and the N.A.S., wanted the full inspection to be retained (Select Committee, 1968, 580). They found it invaluable to headmasters and schools in general and strenuously denied the National Union of Teachers' statement that the full inspection was disturbing and disruptive to schools. Their written evidence concludes with these words:

> The Committee (of the Headmasters' Conference) felt that with re-organization of the educational system of the country on the one hand and the prospect of a new Local Authority structure on the other, there is a serious need for some stabilizing factor on the academic side to keep an eye on the work of schools in different areas and under different schemes of organization. The present Inspectorate is the right body to provide this (H.M.C. Memo, 1968).

The F.E. Inspectorate, although it was combined with the Schools Inspectorate in 1944, retains some special characteristics of its own. Many of its members have had industrial experience. Their teaching experience has been with young people who have left school and who are continuing their education voluntarily (or at least not under statutory compulsion) or with adults. They possess, between them, much highly specialized knowledge and experience and, only rarely do they have any counterparts in the local education service, with the single exception of the Service of Youth. The evidence offered by the A.T.T.I. reflects these differences: 'It is one of the features of F.E. that in most local authority areas the technical college has to exist on its own, without any expert advice from the Local Education Authority. The only body of men able to provide between them the advice . . . that the college requires is H.M. Inspectorate' (A.T.T.I. Memo, 1968, 5). There exists a mass of independent committees which are concerned with F.E. and which are manned largely by industrialists and others with no direct knowledge of education. The A.T.T.I. say: 'The presence of H.M. Inspector as Assessor on these committees is the only safeguard that the colleges have. Without it the situation might be quite disastrous' (A.T.T.I. Memo, 1968, 12). It is not surprising that the A.T.T.I. is the only body which specifically asked for an increase in the numbers of inspectors.

F.E. inspectors have another special function, already briefly referred to in Chapter 2, which must be mentioned again here. Many of the courses which are offered by technical colleges require very expensive equipment and highly specialized staff. It is obviously undesirable, from the economic point of view, that such courses should be multiplied in excess of the need or demand. Someone has to decide which colleges are to have a particular course and which are to be denied. This skilled if invidious task is carried out by H.M.I. who here fills a role of power quite alien from everything else that he does. The Association of Chief Education Officers, though they paid tribute to the fairness and thoroughness shown by H.M.I.s in carrying out this duty, objected very strongly to it but had no very clear suggestion to make for some acceptable alternative (A.C.E.O. Memo., 1968). The A.T.T.I., on the other hand, felt no such objection but were only concerned with the extent to which the inspectors acting in this role were independent or otherwise of the Department. They considered that they were not independent and that this should be acknowledged (Select Committee, 1968, 971). In fact the decision is made by H.M.I. and conveyed to the Department, which almost always accepts it. The *policy* of an economic distribution of technical courses is the Department's responsibility though it was worked out with the advice of the inspectorate.

It may be objected that I have been using, as the Committee did, exclusively establishment opinion, drawn from the senior officers and members of solid organizations, and that I have paid no heed to the views of young teachers or of organizations which are specifically committed to innovation and change. I had to use what was available and, although this was not fully representative of all minority opinion, I am satisfied that it was not so one-sided as to present a distorted view. My own experience of young teachers, which continues to the present moment, is that they are much less shy and inarticulate than many of their predecessors and are not backward in expressing their opinions; and further that they are quite ready to meet H.M.I. as man-to-man, take what he has to offer with unaffected gratitude and ignore what is unacceptable without any sense of guilt. They know how to use him better than many of their parents did.

The evidence offered by Mr Michael Duane, former Headmaster of Risinghill Comprehensive School, requires separate treatment (Select Committee, 1968, 1,114-1,154). Readers of Mrs Berg's book *Death of a School* might expect an attitude of hostility towards the inspectorate in Mr Duane. He made it clear that he looked forward to a time when inspectors would no longer be necessary, though he felt that a great change in society in general would have to come first. He spoke with warm appreciation of one H.M.I. who had helped him and said:

> Looking back on my experience of inspectors, both when they came to schools and when I have seen them at courses, I think that a proportion of them have been of outstanding value in helping teachers to rethink the problems that they are facing day by day and to put them into the broader context of society.

On the other hand he said earlier:

> I have . . . found it surprising that so many of the Department's Inspectors seem to be unaware of the sociological findings in education over the last fifteen years. They would come into schools in very depressed areas without any knowledge, let alone an adequate knowledge, of the effect of social background on the child's capacity to learn and . . . to respond to a disciplined environment and so on.

This statement is difficult to maintain or refute. Mr Duane must necessarily be generalizing from a very small sample. On the other hand, he is certainly right if he thinks that only a very small proportion of the inspectorate have degrees or other qualifications in sociology. Inspectors have worked in slum areas ever since they worked anywhere and this has bred in most, if not all, a great

65

sympathy with the problems of the schools and some knowledge of them. The charge that they have not kept up to date with sociological research may, however, be soundly based. At any rate the Select Committee recommended that there should be 'within the Inspectorate some Inspectors with special knowledge of social developments affecting education'. The Department's comment on this was terse: 'This is already the practice and will be continued' (Observations, 1968).

Some other functions

It is not possible, within the compass of this book, to deal with all the functions and activities of inspectors, which have multiplied in number as well as in intensity since the Second World War. Three, however, require a brief mention.

Refresher courses for teachers on a national scale are a comparatively new development in English education. Before the Second World War most of them were held during the vacation at Oxford or Cambridge, few were for teachers in primary schools, and all were staffed exclusively by H.M. Inspectors. Since 1945 there has been an explosion of courses and, in spite of there being others now in the field, including the Institutes of Education and the Local Education Authorities, the demand for national courses has reached such a level that H.M. Inspectors are no longer able to meet it. In the last five years a number of national courses have been run which had as their object the increase of those capable of staffing courses, by giving to selected teachers the opportunity of participation as staff. There is no question of eliminating inspectors from these duties but rather of relieving them of the sole burden.

The organization and running of a national course for teachers is a very exacting task and one in which a variety of demands is made upon the staff. They have to become teachers again and they have to keep up their reading and study and their acquaintance with modern development. No inspector who was out of touch with the classroom or with the subject of the course could hope to be invited to take part and, since nearly every inspector cherishes such a hope, the courses are in some sense a safeguard against inspectorial barrenness. Some inspectors are in such demand that it has been necessary to fix a limit to the number of courses in which any one man or woman can take part in a year. This has the beneficial effect of producing a constant search for new blood, and newly joined inspectors can often make their earliest contribution in this field. In addition to the national courses there are courses run by Local Education Authorities and teachers' associations in most of which H.M. Inspectors will be found taking part. Some years ago it was calculated that about 7 per cent of inspectorial time was spent on courses and this was judged to be about right, since the course, like everything else that an inspector does, depends for its usefulness upon the fact that the major part of his time is spent in school. It is probably nearer 10 per cent now and it would be most undesirable that it should rise above this.

In 1964, a new phenomenon appeared on the educational scene—the Schools Council for the Development of the Curriculum and Examinations. This sprang from a growing feeling that, although it was wrong that the central authority should exercise any control over curriculum or methods, there was nevertheless a place for some kind of national organization which would study curriculum problems, and undertake development projects. A small forerunner

67

of the Council, the Curriculum Study Group, which had been established in 1961 inside the Department had aroused among teachers deep suspicion that the D.E.S. was going to try to exercise control. Although this suspicion was quite unfounded, it was felt that an organization under the control of teachers would be better than one, however innocent its intentions, which was inside the Department. The Schools Council was therefore established, after a lengthy series of meetings in which all interests took part. The Select Committee very properly inquired into the possibility that the Council had taken over, or would shortly do so, some responsibilities hitherto discharged by H.M. Inspectorate. It did not appear in the evidence that this was really so and my own experience confirms this (Select Committee, 1968, 125). The activities of the Council clearly touch those of the Inspectorate at many points and even dovetail into them, and the rapidly developing Teachers' Centres form a point at which H.M. Inspectors and Council meet, but the two organizations are essentially complementary. The work of the inspectorate will be greatly enhanced by the work of the Council and one witness to the Committee, and one not very friendly to the inspectorate either, went so far as to say that the Council could not exist without the inspectorate (Select Committee, 1968, 1,103). Inspectors sit on all its sub-committees, one of its joint secretaries has so far always been an H.M.I., and H.M.I.s are associated, sometimes to the extent of almost total secondment, with all its projects. At the time when the Select Committee sat, about ninety inspectors were involved in the Council's work, of whom six were seconded full or part-time (Select Committee, 1968, 476-7).

For many years, even before the First World War, it has been the policy of the Department to send some H.M.

Inspectors abroad, either for study or to give active assistance in education in other countries. In the thirties a number of interesting reports were published as a result of these visits. Latterly they have increased, and a small number of H.M. Inspectors go abroad every year for short periods to visit schools and take part in international courses and conferences. From developing countries, chiefly in Africa, come constant requests for the loan of H.M. Inspectors for more prolonged periods. If all these requests were met the inspectorate at home would be seriously depleted (Select Committee, 1968, 219). The complement allows for up to six overseas secondments at a time. In addition, the inspectorate is responsible for the inspection of Forces education at home and overseas and of the education of Forces children in all foreign stations. This responsibility has recently declined, but it is still heavy enough in Germany to require quite lengthy periodical visits by two or three inspectors at once.

The Universities, except for their teacher training and extra-mural departments, are entirely outside the scope of H.M. Inspectorate, but, with this single exception, there is no part of the educational field, maintained or independent, academic or vocational, juvenile or adult, compulsory or voluntary, with which H.M.I.s are not concerned. They are omnipresent, and though they would never claim or aspire to omniscience, they do know, between them, more about English education than any other body in the country.

5

The inspectorate in the future

The Select Committee, having heard and read the evidence, wrote a report and made recommendations. This, by kind permission of H.M. Stationery Office, is printed as an appendix to this book, together with the Department's comments (Observations, 1968). I hope that the latter will adopt some but not all of the Committee's suggestions. All I can do here is to set down some of what seem to me to be the features which it is essential to preserve, whatever new look the inspectorate is to wear and whatever the changes in the educational system which may bear upon the inspectorate and its functions. The National Union of Teachers, at the conclusion of its oral evidence, expressed the hope that a day would come when H.M. Inspectorate would be replaced by a (presumably similar) body, responsible to the teaching profession alone and not to the state, but they admitted that that day was yet far off (Select Committee, 1968, 773-4). I think myself that it is very far off indeed and beyond it I cannot look, though I believe that a teacher inspectorate would have to adopt many, if not all, of the principles which H.M. Inspectorate has learned in the 130 years of its existence. It might even begin by appointing all the ex-H.M.I.s to its ranks.

The features that it is essential to preserve are these:

1. The independence of the inspectorate in the terms in which I have defined it in chapter 4. The inalienable professional independence must be supported by the way in which the inspectorate is organized. Whether it is national, or some kind of mixture of national and regional, it must be a separate corps under its own S.C.I. whose status must be such as will ensure that professional independence will be unimpaired and that inspectors will not be at the beck and call of national or regional governments. Such an organization should also make it possible for the inspectorate to preserve, indeed to foster, the individuality and even the eccentricity of its members. They should never think of themselves as officials or behave like officials, but rather as colleagues of each other and of those they inspect.

2. The quality of the inspectorate cannot be too high. If ever it became a body of second-rate uninspired and uninspiring ex-school teachers I should like to see it die. It must draw on the best that the teaching world has to offer and for that reason, if for no other, it must not grow in size. In 1958 it numbered 531 (England and Wales). In 1959 it dropped to 520, by the inspectors' own wish and recommendation. Now it is 543, owing to the increasing demands made upon it, yet it has had to drop, almost completely, the full inspection. I hope it will never top 600.

3. Conversely the inspectorate must not be so small that it cannot spend most of its time in school. Here I agree most strongly with the National Union of Teachers. The Committee recognize the importance of this but still recommend a reduction in numbers,

mainly in the expectation that the larger units of local government which the Maud Committee has recommended will be able to appoint their own inspectorates, but also because teachers are better qualified than they were and need inspectors less (Select Committee Report, 1968, 42). This fails to take account of the fact that the reduction has really taken place already, in the sense that, unlike every other body in education and out of it, the inspectorate has scarcely grown. As long ago as 1945 a joint committee of office and inspectorate estimated that over 600 inspectors would be needed to meet the obligations then existing. For its present duties the inspectorate is badly undermanned and even if those duties are reduced, which will not be easy, the numbers will still be barely adequate to perform those that remain. Too small an inspectorate, a miniature corps *d'élite*, experts who cerebrated, researched and preached doctrine would, in my view, be a menace to everything that is best in English education; its informality, its friendliness, its encouragement of individual initiative, its pragmatic approach.

In conclusion, what are they to be called? 'Inspectors' is generally disliked, but no one has suggested an alternative which has been generally acclaimed. I am rather attracted by the term 'Visitor' with which the National Union of Teachers apparently toyed (Select Committee, 1968, 742), but I doubt whether it would catch on. 'Adviser' or 'Advisor', however you spell it, is more one-sided than 'Inspector'. Etymologically, for what this is worth, the two words are almost identical in meaning (*inspicere*—to look in, *advidere*—to look at). But whatever they are,

are they to be 'Her Majesty's'? This is doubtless mainly a matter of sentiment, but sentiment is important. The words emphasize that education is not simply the concern of the ratepayer or taxpayer, the local authority, or the Government or even Parliament, but of the country as a whole, which is symbolized by the Crown.

Suggestions for further reading

The main sources of information may be found in the bibliography. I have already expressed my admiration of Edmonds's *The School Inspector* and Nancy Ball's *H.M. Inspectorate 1839-1849*. These two books together provide the most complete historical account available. Matthew Arnold's *Reports on Elementary Schools 1852–1882* is worth reading as a period piece and as exhibiting an enlightenment which was far from common in Victorian days. Sneyd-Kinnersley's *H.M.I.* is amusing in parts and revealing at many points of the evils of payment-by-results and the day-to-day life of inspectors in the latter part of the nineteenth century. Three other books of inspectorial reminiscences may be mentioned: *To return to all that* (A. P. Graves), *Memories of a School Inspector* (A. J. Swinburne)—both out of print—and, much the best of all, *An Inspector's Testament* by F. H. Spencer, English Universities Press 1938.

Bibliography

Official reports and documents

Association of Education Officers (1968) *Memorandum submitted to Select Committee*, H.M.S.O.
Association of Teachers in Technical Institutions (1968) *Memorandum submitted to Select Committee*, H.M.S.O.
Council (1840-1) *Minutes of the Council.*
Headmasters' Conference (1968) *Memorandum submitted to Select Committee*, H.M.S.O.
National Union of Teachers (1968) *Memorandum submitted to Select Committee*, H.M.S.O.
Department of Education and Science (1968) *Observations on the recommendations on Part I of the Report from the Select Committee*, H.M.S.O.
Select Committee (1968) *Report on Education and Science, Part One, Her Majesty's Inspectorate*, H.M.S.O.

Books, pamphlets and reports

ARNOLD, M. (1908) *Reports on Elementary Schools 1852–1882* (edited F. S. Marvin, H.M.I.), H.M.S.O.
BALL, N. (1963) *Her Majesty's Inspectorate 1839–1849*, Educational Monograph No. 6, Oliver & Boyd for Birmingham University.
BOOTHROYD, H. E. (1923) *A History of the Inspectorate*. Privately printed for Inspectors' Association.
EDMONDS, E. L. (1962) *The School Inspector*, Routledge & Kegan Paul.
GRAVES, A. P. (1930) *To return to all that*, Cape.
HOLMES, E. (1910) *Memorandum No. 21*, 6 January.
KAY-SHUTTLEWORTH, SIR JAMES (1862) *Four periods of public Education*, Longmans.

BIBLIOGRAPHY

MORRIS, THE REV. M. C. F. (1922) *Yorkshire Reminiscences*, Oxford University Press.

NEWCASTLE (1860) *Royal Commission on the State of Popular Education in England, under the chairmanship of the Duke of Newcastle*, H.M.S.O.

PLOWDEN, LADY (1967) *Children in their Primary Schools*, Report of the Central Advisory Council, under the Chairmanship of Lady Plowden. 2 vols., H.M.S.O.

SNEYD-KINNERSLEY, E. M. (1908) *H.M.I.*, Macmillan.

Appendix I

A select committee of the House of Commons was appointed on 22 February 1968 'to consider the activities of the Department of Education and Science and the Scottish Education Department and to report thereon'. Part One of the Report was published in July 1968 and is printed here by permission of H.M. Stationery Office. It deals with Her Majesty's Inspectorate (England and Wales).

The Committee met eighteen times in all, thirteen times in public, and took oral evidence from a large number of individuals and organizations, besides receiving thirty memoranda and twenty-two papers (i.e. factual information) from a variety of sources.

REPORT

The Select Committee appointed to consider the activities of the Department of Education and Science and the Scottish Education Department have agreed to the following Report:—

PART I. HER MAJESTY'S INSPECTORATE (ENGLAND AND WALES)

I. INTRODUCTION

1. Bearing in mind the limitation of choice explained in our Third Special Report, we decided this Session to enquire into H.M. Inspectorate, setting up a Sub-Committee to deal with the Scottish aspect of the enquiry.

2. A list of the witnesses we saw is at p. xxiii and a list of the Memoranda and Papers we received at pp. xxv, xxvi.

3. We visited two teachers' centres run by the Inner London Education Authority.

II. THE BACKGROUND

4. In 1833 Parliament voted £20,000 towards the erection of school buildings for the education of the poor and in 1839 a Committee of the Privy Council on Education was created to administer the grants. This was the start of H.M. Inspectorate, a watchdog to ensure the proper spending of public money.

5. The Secretary to that Committee, Sir James Kay-Shuttleworth, was not content with this negative function. He advised the Inspectors that:

> . . . it is of the utmost consequence that you should bear in mind that this inspection is not intended as a means of exercising control, but of affording assistance; that it is not to be regarded as operating for the restraint of local efforts, but for their encouragement; and that its chief objects will not be attained without the co-operation of the school committees—the Inspector

having no power to interfere, and not being instructed to offer any advice, or information excepting where it is invited.

6. However, in 1861, as the result of a Commission appointed in 1858 to examine methods of extending sound cheap education, a code was promulgated which made grants dependent on examinations. This system of pay-ment-by-results was gradually modified but it provoked opposition which continued into the twentieth century and may even have some effect today.

7. Subsection (2) of section 77 of the Education Act 1944 now provides:

It shall be the duty of the Minister to cause inspections to be made of every educational establishment at such intervals as appear to him to be appropriate, and to cause a special inspection of any such establishment to be made whenever he considers such an inspection desirable. . . . Provided that the Minister shall not be required by virtue of this subsection to cause inspections to be made of any educational establishment during any period during which he is satisfied that suitable arrangements are in force for the inspection of that establishment otherwise than in accordance with this subsection.

These are unequivocal words. The Minister is required to cause inspections to be made of every educational estab-lishment at appropriate intervals, or to satisfy himself that there are other suitable arrangements.

8. In 1956, the Inspectorate reviewed its role by a work-ing party under the then Senior Chief Inspector, Sir Martin Roseveare. The working party confined their enquiry

within the Inspectorate and held no discussions with the education authorities or others about the conclusions they reached. They themselves recommended that steps should be taken at the proper time to explain their proposed changes to local education authorities and other institutions as well as to teachers; the Permanent Secretary had no idea whether this had been done (Q. 95) but the Secretary of the Association of Local Education Committees was very clear that the changes had not been explained to his Association (Q. 248). Later some attempts have been made to tell teachers and others about the changes (Q. 213) but more could have and should have been done.

9. H.M. Inspectors are not the only education inspectors, for many are employed by local authorities—indeed, London has had its own inspectors ever since it became an education authority. Subsection (3) of section 77 of the Education Act 1944 provides:

> Any local education authority may cause an inspection to be made of any educational establishment maintained by the authority, and such inspections shall be made by officers appointed by the local education authority.

III. The Present

A. *Establishment*

10. In 1956 there were 547 Inspectors in England and Wales; today, at an estimated overall cost of £2,892,000, there are 543. The Roseveare Report recommended a decrease to about 513; that this was not achieved was ascribed to a general accumulation of work.

11. To a question about the size of the Inspectorate the Permanent Secretary replied: 'If I was asked whether we

could use an Inspectorate of 1,000 instead of 500 I would say Yes; on the other hand we could get by on 250 but 500 seems a reasonable sort of figure in present circumstances' (Q. 54) and the Senior Chief Inspector found 'something about the Inspectorate, because it was about 500 people, which was worth preserving and which would soon be lost if we increased the number very much' (Q. 16).

12. Now, as in 1956, 500 seems to be regarded as the right number and, with difficulty, the work has been made to fit it; we think that on the contrary the number should be made to fit the work.

13. To carry out its statutory duty of inspecting every educational establishment the Inspectorate would require a large increase, for its establishment has not kept pace with the much larger numbers of schoolchildren and Further Education students and the increasing complexity of education since the war.

B. *Recruitment*

14. Recruitment to H.M. Inspectorate is mainly from teachers, often from heads of department or head teachers, the exceptions usually being where technical or special knowledge is required. The number of specialists is increasing, but only Further Education Inspectors have much experience in industry. Inspectors are no longer recruited almost entirely from the public schools, but from a wide range of establishments. Some teachers, however, particularly non-graduates from primary and secondary schools, are not well represented, and the recruitment of Further Education Inspectors and of science and mathematics candidates is specially difficult.

15. Vacancies are advertised nationally, the first qualities sought in otherwise suitable applicants being modesty, enthusiasm and the absence of the purely administrative mind, together with powers of persuasion and of giving advice (Q. 5). In Wales, a knowledge of Welsh is desirable but not essential.

16. There are comparatively few women and the Senior Chief Inspector admitted to the Inspectorate being 'masculine at the top' (Q. 14). The reasons for this are largely practical. The situation is expected to improve, although the number of women candidates is small.

C. *Organization*

17. The higher officers of the Inspectorate are concentrated in London, but the field work is spread over the country as a whole. The areas in which Inspectors work are not the economic planning regions; it is considered more important to conform with local authority boundaries.

18. Communications within the Inspectorate are through a panel system supplemented by conferences, but within the department itself methods of diffusion of information are 'a bit primitive' (Q. 122). Consultation with the Planning Branch is through a Joint Planning Committee, but a former Senior Chief Inspector felt that there was a danger of advice from the Inspectorate getting 'lost' (QQ. 175, 182). He suggested as a remedy that the Senior Chief Inspector should rank neither above, nor below, but with the higher civil servants (Q. 179). Although the Inspectorate is a part of the Department its capacity for giving independent advice should be carefully safeguarded.

19. The structure of the Inspectorate is set out in para-

graphs 2 and 6 of the departmental memorandum[1] and the numbers in the English divisions are on page 7. In practice the senior posts are filled by promotion from the main grade (Q. 2) and there is little or no transference between the Inspectorate and the rest of the Department.

20. The relationship of the Inspectorate with the Inner London Educational Authority, which has a substantial inspectorate of its own, is good: the roles of the two inspectorates are complementary (QQ. 223, 398), but it became apparent in the course of our enquiry that there are some local education authorities and inspectorates who hesitate to consult H.M. Inspectors when their help would obviously be valuable. Local inspectors have detailed local knowledge while H.M. Inspectors have country-wide experience, and the lack of formal relationship between them should not impair their co-operation.

D. *Particular functions*

(a) *Formal Inspections*

21. A formal inspection consists of a team of Inspectors visiting a school for several days, enquiring into every aspect of its work and examining its buildings and appurtenances; this is followed by a comprehensive written report. Such inspections used to be made about every five years, but the intervals between inspections have never been defined (Q. 65) and the present intervals cannot be given (QQ. 67, 68).

22. Reports following formal inspections, before being 'solemnly buried in the cellars at Curzon Street' (Q. 56), are made available to governing bodies and to local educa-

[1] Minutes of Evidence, pp. 1, 2.

tion authorities, a representative of whom found them useful (QQ. 827, 832), but the primary purpose of such inspections was said by a former Senior Chief Inspector to be to report to the Department (Q. 200). We studied several of these reports, on various types of school. Although carefully prepared, they did not all seem to serve any purpose commensurate with the time spent on them.

23. Although formal inspections are still made, there is now no rota for them. The work is increasingly done by informal visits (the last instruction was that an Inspector should try to visit his schools once every five terms), by sampling and by surveys of particular aspects of education over a number of establishments. In some schools a new type of 'miniature' inspection has been used (Q. 578).

24. Most of our witnesses agreed that the old type of formal inspection is outdated, but they were not all agreed on the need for formal inspections of a newer type. Opinions ranged from 'quite a bit to come out of it' (Q. 207) to 'dead, no longer necessary' (Q. 300).

(b) *Independent Schools*

25. Independent schools which seek recognition[1] as efficient are formally inspected. All other independent schools have to be registered and visited regularly. All independent boarding schools are now inspected to ensure that they reach the standard required for recognition and the Department are considering provision for the appoint-

[1] There is some confusion in the public mind about the difference between 'recognized' and 'registered'. The first means that the school has been found efficient after inspection by H.M. Inspectorate; the second means little more than that the school exists. We share the view that the Department should re-consider the two terms and try to devise more informative ones.

ment of 19 more Inspectors for this work.

26. It would help if some inspections were less elaborate; a witness from the Incorporated Association of Preparatory Schools said (Q. 565) that they would not mind if Inspectors came frequently without making a formal inspection. The local inspectors could assist in this work, although witnesses from both the Incorporated Association of Preparatory Schools and the Headmasters' Conference said that they would not be happy with inspections carried out by local inspectorates (QQ. 536, 586) and stressed the value they placed on H.M. Inspectorate.

(c) *Further Education*

27. Some 90 Inspectors deal with the work in 700 Colleges of Further Education and are also responsible for inspecting non-vocational work provided by university extramural departments, the W.E.A., the Youth Employment Service, the Youth Service and in penal establishments. The Inspectorate has two main tasks: first, as in schools, to advise classroom teachers, heads of departments and principals; secondly, to play an important part, fundamentally different from that in schools, in relation to the administrative side of the service, including the allocation of courses to Colleges which necessarily involves policy decisions (Q. 968).

(d) *Special Schools*

28. To deal with special schools for handicapped children and with approved schools (in collaboration with the Home Office) a former Senior Chief Inspector thought the Inspectorate was quite well manned, with a small but

strong team (Q. 171).

29. General approval of their work was expressed in a memorandum from the College of Teachers of the Blind; the National College of Teachers of the Deaf thought the staff of four Inspectors gave an excellent service, which they would like to see expanded; the Association of Teachers of Maladjusted Children considered that the Inspectors' intentions were of the best but also recommended expanded provision; the Guild of Teachers of Backward Children thought that at least ten per cent of the Inspectorate should have experience of children with special needs; the National Union of Teachers felt that there is room for 'a few additional specialist Inspectors in this field of education'.

(e) *In-service training*

30. A basic task of H.M. Inspectorate is to help teachers to teach better. Many teachers will have little chance of meeting H.M. Inspectors, but the in-service courses run for teachers by the Inspectorate are clearly popular and useful. The extension of teachers' centres give an opportunity for teachers to meet local authority inspectors in a setting removed from the inquisitorial atmosphere of old style inspection, and could also provide a useful forum for discussion with H.M. Inspectors.

E. *The Schools Council for the Curriculum and Examinations*

31. The Schools Council, which has been in operation for more than three years, replaced the Curriculum Study Group. Its financial resources are £675,000 a year from

the local authorities and £100,000 from the Department, which also provides staff and services, a total cost of some £1¼ million. Its main function is the promotion of research and development; its field primary and secondary education; its purpose to develop discussion among industry, teachers and the Inspectorate. It is not concerned with major policy.

32. Generally, witnesses were in favour of the Council, although one from the National Union of Teachers said doubts had been voiced about its independence (Q. 735). Its chief difficulty seems to lie in evaluating and disseminating the results of the work it does; a Joint Secretary, himself an H.M.I., thought that in the schools where development projects are tried progress was slow but positive, and that later the problem would be that of transmitting the effect of its work to schools in general. It is clearly important that teachers should be given as much information as possible.

33. The Schools Council commissions research into new methods and evaluates them; H.M. Inspectors advise on their use; the teacher decides on their benefit to him. Two difficulties, however, arise: first, it is doubtful whether all such research should be concentrated in one central body whose funds are provided by central and local education authorities; secondly, teachers fear that such a system might be the precursor of central control of curricula.

F. *Local Inspectorates*

34. The local inspectorates began in response to the need to provide supervision for such additional practical subjects as handicrafts, domestic science and physical education.

Their Association was founded in 1918. Their responsibility has expanded rapidly and there are now possibly some 2,000 local inspectors, organizers and advisers. Most local inspectors have been teachers; their status and pay (which is lower than that of H.M. Inspectors) vary between different authorities. Broadly, the local inspectorates reflect the size of the local education authorities. The Inner London Education Authority has a staff of 77 and Lancashire 57, but smaller authorities such as Bury, Great Yarmouth and Worcester each have only one officer and Merthyr Tydfil none. The Department foresaw a time, fifty years hence, when local inspectorates would be adequate to undertake all inspection work (QQ. 62, 63, 70) and one witness gave 15 as the minimum number of inspectors for a local authority area (Q. 275). If the re-organization of local government results in a smaller number of larger authorities the process could be quickened.

IV. RECENT DEVELOPMENTS AND FUTURE TRENDS

35. In discharging their functions H.M. Inspectorate have always been faced with a dilemma. Appointed to safeguard the spending of public money, Inspectors were advised by Sir James Kay-Shuttleworth that inspection was 'not intended as a means of exercising control', but, indeed, of encouraging local efforts, incurring probably increased expenditure. The dilemma has persisted. Section 77 of the Education Act 1944 clearly imposes a duty on the Secretary of State to cause inspections, but does not define their purpose and, in spite of the declaratory words of Section 1 of the Act, the primary responsibility for education lies with the local education authorities. After all, they build the schools and employ the teachers. Neither claims direct

responsibility for the content of education.

36. The recognition of local responsibility has encouraged the local discharge of that responsibility. In one form or another, there has been a rapid growth in the number of local authority inspectors, advisers and organizers, so that today there are probably four or five of them to each H.M. Inspector. This development ought seriously to affect the establishment and functions of the Inspectorate.

37. The role of H.M. Inspectorate has indeed changed considerably. Inspection itself is no longer regarded as its main function and the statutory obligation on the Secretary of State to cause inspections of all educational establishments has for long been disregarded (Q. 209). Formal inspections of maintained schools are still held but at long intervals, haphazardly, and for no purpose that is clearly understood. H.M. Inspectors regard themselves in the main as advisers and consider such inspections as they hold incidental to their advisory work.

38. As the work of inspection by H.M. Inspectorate has decreased, so the advisory work has expanded, but at the same time other advisory services have been provided. Many local inspectorates are equally concerned in affording advice and equally regard themselves more as advisers than inspectors. More important, when the Department's Curriculum Study Group was translated into the Schools Council for the Curriculum and Examinations, the major responsibility for advice on the curriculum was thereby transferred from the Department to the Council, a development which again calls for a reassessment of the work of H.M. Inspectorate.

39. Thus the Inspectorate do not now work alone. The work is shared both by the local inspectorates and, through the Schools Council, by the teachers themselves.

89

Moreover we must recognize that as the local authorities have become increasingly jealous of their responsibility and the teachers increasingly conscious of their professional status so the share of H.M. Inspectorate will inevitably continue to diminish.

40. Throughout our enquiry, we heard a good deal of evidence about the independence of the Inspectorate. We do not consider appointment by Her Majesty in Council to be of any great significance, although we recognize that it 'delights the people who enjoy it' (Q. 55). That H.M. Inspectorate is wholly independent of the Department is a myth: 'The Department and the Inspectorate are a very integrated body' (Q. 119). We noticed that the Divisional Inspector represents the Department on the Regional Economic Planning Boards and we believe that Inspectors are generally accepted as spokesmen of the Department. Although their advice is sought within the Department we consider that the arrangements for both inviting and affording proper consideration of that advice could be greatly improved. We do not, however, feel that the relationship of the Inspectorate to the Department prejudices the independence of an Inspector where he is clearly expressing a personal judgement.

41. In view of the growing emphasis on the advisory nature of its functions, many witnesses suggested that the title of H.M. Inspectorate should be changed. The Inspectors themselves do not want this and there was no general agreement on a new title. We therefore make no recommendation.

42. We cannot accept that, whatever the circumstances, an establishment of about 500 is right for the Inspectorate. On the contrary, we believe that it should be the subject of a realistic review. The Inspectorate should, in general,

cease full-scale inspections and accept that the major responsibility for inspections should rest with the local education authorities where their inspectorates are adequate. This does not mean completely abandoning inspecting by H.M. Inspectors, for at present some education authorities are incapable of discharging such responsibility. Moreover, teachers see inspection by local inspectorates as inspection by their employers and the possibility of inspection by H.M. Inspectorate should remain as a safeguard. Further, we accept inspection as incidental to the advisory services of H.M. Inspectorate. With regard to these advisory services, we consider that much of the work at present undertaken by the Inspectorate should be done in co-operation with the Schools Council and the increasing number of teachers' centres, the role of H.M. Inspectors being to generalize the best practice in education and to act as a catalytic agent to promote improvement. Furthermore, it would be unfortunate to lose the advantages of a professional element within the Department. All this, however, does not justify the present establishment. What is needed is a smaller, possibly more highly specialized Inspectorate, more closely related to its changed functions and more in touch with social developments affecting education.

43. We believe that provision ought to be made to allow and encourage Inspectors to refresh their teaching experience during their service and some reduction in the effective strength of the Inspectorate could be made immediately by making provision for Inspectors to teach in schools, colleges and departments of education for a period. This, incidentally, would help to bridge the noticeable gap in English and Welsh education between the training of teachers and the practice of teaching.

44. In the case of independent schools the special considerations of 'registration' and 'recognition as efficient' apply. As we have said, the complement of H.M. Inspectors is being increased by 19 for the inspection of independent boarding schools. In our opinion, before proceeding with these appointments, the Department ought to have considered other measures. There should be far greater flexibility in the inspection of independent schools. In many cases 'miniature' or less formal inspections would be adequate. We saw a formal written report on a well known public school which seemed to us a profligate use of the time of a hard pressed Inspectorate. Moreover, we consider that some of the work (for instance that relating to premises and accommodation) could well be delegated to local authority inspectorates, and that specialist members of the local inspectorates could be invited to assist in inspections. Apart from inspection, the independent schools benefit from the advisory service of H.M. Inspectorate and this should continue.

45. Special considerations also apply in Further Education, which is at a different stage of development from that of the schools and complicated by the difficulties caused by the changing frontiers between Further and Higher Education. At present many local education authorities are not large enough to maintain more than one or two Colleges of Further Education and some courses are so limited that they are held in only a few widely scattered centres. It appears to us that H.M. Inspectorate should not work in isolation but that they should consider with the local authorities how the work can be made both more efficient, avoiding unnecessary duplication, and adapted to changing circumstances. As with the schools, we believe that essentially the value of H.M. Inspectorate depends

upon a real and active participation with the local education authorities and the teachers themselves.

V. Recommendations

46. A. *The Work*

(1) Section 77 of the Education Act 1944 should be amended to replace the duty at present imposed on the Secretary of State by the *right* to cause inspections to be made.

(2) Full-scale formal inspections by H.M. Inspectorate of maintained schools and the formal written reports which accompany them should be discontinued, save in exceptional circumstances; in future, Inspectors should rely on informal visits. The Department should make a clear statement to this effect.

(3) Where they are adequate, a greater share of inspection should be left to the inspectorates of local authorities and closer liaison between them and H.M. Inspectorate should be established. The Secretary of State should, however, retain his right to require a formal inspection of a school by H.M. Inspectorate, particularly if so requested by a local education authority or a teachers' organization.

(4) There should be much greater flexibility in the inspection of independent schools, particularly, where it is appropriate, by the use of 'miniature' and less formal inspections. Some of the work could be delegated to local authority inspectorates, but this should not affect the advisory service given to the independent schools by H.M. Inspectorate.

(5) Area or regional reports should be prepared by H.M. Inspectors and published; and a summary of them should be published in an annual report.

B. *The Staff*

(6) The field organization of H.M. Inspectorate should conform with the economic planning regions.

(7) The status of the Senior Chief Inspector should be raised to the equivalent of deputy secretary, with corresponding changes in other grades. Movement within the Department should be made easier and the salary structure reviewed, so that Inspectors would have greater opportunities of reaching the highest posts in the Civil Service.

(8) Although the system of recruitment appears generally adequate, particular attention should be paid in future to securing a better balance of recruits of the right calibre with experience in primary, all forms of secondary, Further and Higher Education and in local inspectorates, and to the need to have within the Inspectorate some Inspectors with special knowledge of social developments affecting education.

(9) Provision should be made to allow Inspectors, during their service, to be seconded to teaching posts in schools, colleges and departments of education, and this should be embodied in their contract of service.

C. *Further Education*

(10) As the work of the Inspectorate in Further Education differs from that in schools and is at a different stage of development, a joint working party, including representatives of local authorities, should be set up to examine what alterations are needed in this branch of the Inspectorate, how recruitment can be improved, particularly with regard to specialists, and how the work should be adapted to changing circumstances.

D. *The Schools Council*

(11) Now that the Schools Council has become an established body, H.M. Inspectors seconded to it should be transferred from the establishment of the Department to that of the Council. Better provision should be made for the dissemination by the Council of the results of its research and development.

E. *Research*

(12) Educational research is clearly important to the work of H.M. Inspectorate. The Department should consider with interested parties the improvement and co-ordination of such research so that information is more readily available to those who most need it, the teachers.

VI. CONCLUSION

47. Throughout our inquiry we have found that the work of H.M. Inspectorate is widely appreciated. We share that view and welcome the emphasis on the advisory rather than the inquisitorial aspect of that work. In our opinion, however, the Department has failed sufficiently to recognize this evolution and failed to appreciate the effect upon H.M. Inspectorate of the growth of the local inspectorates, the development of the Schools Council and the enhanced status of the teaching profession. We believe that the effect of the acceptance of our recommendations would be an appreciable decrease in the numbers of H.M. Inspectorate, a clear recognition of its changed function and a more realistic view of its organization.

Appendix 2

OBSERVATIONS BY THE DEPARTMENT OF EDUCATION AND SCIENCE ON THE RECOMMENDATIONS IN PART I OF THE REPORT FROM THE SELECT COMMITTEE ON EDUCATION AND SCIENCE, SESSION 1967–68 (Commd. 3,860)

1 Section 77 of the Education Act, 1944 should be amended to replace the duty at present imposed on the Secretary of State by the right to cause inspections to be made.

OBSERVATION

This recommendation is noted.

2 Full-scale formal inspections by H.M. Inspectorate of maintained schools and the formal written reports which accompany them should be discontinued, save in exceptional circumstances; in future, Inspectors should rely on informal visits. The Department should make a clear statement to this effect.

OBSERVATION

At present there is a wide variety of visits representing

all degrees of formality and elaboration from the traditional full inspection to a brief call by a single Inspector. Many visits which are not full inspections nevertheless involved rigorous appraisal by a number of Inspectors of one or more aspects of school work. The balance is shifting away from full inspections followed by formal reports and will continue to do so; in accordance with an instruction issued to Inspectors in April, 1968, they now take place only for some special reason.

3 *Where they are adequate, a greater share of inspection should be left to the inspectorates of local authorities and closer liaison between them and H.M. Inspectorate should be established. The Secretary of State should, however, retain his right to require a formal inspection of a school by H.M. Inspectorate, particularly if so requested by a local education authority or a teachers' organization.*

OBSERVATION

Liaison with the inspectorates of local authorities, where these exist in any strength, is already taking place but it is agreed that it should become closer. The possibilities of this are being explored with some suitable authorities.

4 *There should be much greater flexibility in the inspection of independent schools, particularly, where it is appropriate, by the use of 'miniature' and less formal inspections. Some of the work could be delegated to local authority inspectorates, but this should not affect the advisory service given to the independent schools by H.M. Inspectorate.*

OBSERVATION

There is a wide variety of independent schools. For some, informal or miniature inspections may well be sufficient, but this must be subject to the need to maintain uniform national standards for recognition as efficient and the (at present) lower requirements for continued registration of schools under Part III of the Education Act 1944. It is intended to seek to raise the minimum standard of all independent schools over a period of years to that for recognition as efficient, and a start is being made in relation to boarding schools. Failure to attain the standard for recognition as efficient within a period of a year or two after initial inspection and advice from the Department will lead to notices of complaint under Part III of the Act. Similar considerations need to be borne in mind when a school is first seeking recognition or its claims to remain recognized are in jeopardy.

In the context of Part III of the Act, whether on the standards of tolerability hitherto accepted or the new higher standards now to be used, inspection has to be meticulously thorough, yielding evidence that will, if necessary, be accepted by an independent schools tribunal. This work could not be delegated to local authorities without a change in the law. Maintenance of uniform standards is increasingly important in this field and special teams of expert and experienced Inspectors have had to be developed.

5 *Area or regional reports should be prepared by H.M. Inspectors and published; and a summary of them should be published in an annual report.*

OBSERVATION

National surveys of some aspects of education have already been published. Surveys of aspects of work over an area have been steadily increasing in number and the possibility of publishing some is being considered.

6 The field organization of H.M. Inspectorate should conform with the economic planning regions.

OBSERVATION

This is being considered.

7 The status of the Senior Chief Inspector should be raised to the equivalent of deputy secretary, with corresponding changes in other grades. Movement within the Department should be made easier and the salary structure reviewed, so that Inspectors would have greater opportunities of reaching the highest posts in the Civil Service.

OBSERVATION

This is being considered.

8 Although the system of recruitment appears generally adequate, particular attention should be paid in future to securing a better balance of recruits, of the right calibre with experience in Primary, all forms of Secondary, Further and Higher Education and in local inspectorates, and to the need to have within the Inspectorate some Inspectors with special knowledge of social developments affecting education.

99

Observation

This is already the practice and will be continued.

9 *Provision should be made to allow Inspectors, during their service, to be seconded to teaching posts in schools, colleges and departments of education, and this should be embodied in their contract of service.*

Observation

In recent years two Inspectors have been seconded for short periods, one to a college of education and one to a university department of education. The main practical difficulty arises from differences in salary and this would be among the main problems involved in any general scheme provided for in the conditions of service. This matter is, however, being considered.

10 *As the work of the Inspectorate in Further Education differs from that in schools and is at a different stage of development, a joint working party, including representatives of local authorities, should be set up to examine what alterations are needed in this branch of the Inspectorate, how recruitment can be improved, particularly with regard to specialists, and how the work should be adapted to changing circumstances.*

Observation

The work of, and recruitment into, the group of Inspectors concerned with Further Education will be reviewed; and in the course of the study local education authorities and others concerned will be consulted.

11 Now that the Schools Council has become an established body, H.M. Inspectors seconded to it should be transferred from the establishment of the Department to that of the Council. Better provision should be made for the dissemination by the Council of the results of its research and development.

OBSERVATION

The Schools Council does not at present have its own establishment of staff; staff serving the Council are members of the staff of the Department. This system is under consideration at present and the position of H.M. Inspectors working with the Council will be among the questions arising. Dissemination of the results of the Council's research and development is a matter for the Council.

12 Educational research is clearly important to the work of H.M. Inspectorate. The Department should consider with interested parties the improvement and co-ordination of such research so that information is more readily available to those who most need it, the teachers.

OBSERVATION

This recommendation is accepted.